Charlotte Brontë

THE PROFILES IN LITERATURE SERIES

GENERAL EDITOR : B. C. SOUTHAM, M.A., B.LITT. (OXON.)
Formerly Department of English, Westfield College, University of London

Volumes in the series include

CHARLES DICKENS	Martin Fido, *University of Leeds*
HENRY FIELDING	C. J. Rawson, *University of Warwick*
JAMES JOYCE	Arnold Goldman, *University of Sussex*
HERMAN MELVILLE	D. E. S. Maxwell, *University of Ibadan*
THOMAS LOVE PEACOCK	Carl Dawson, *University of California*
SAMUEL RICHARDSON	A. M. Kearney, *Chorley College of Education*
WALTER SCOTT	Robin Mayhead, *University of Ghana*
JONATHAN SWIFT	Kathleen Williams, *University of California*
ZOLA	Philip Walker, *University of California*

Charlotte Brontë

by *Arthur Pollard*

Professor of English in the
University of Hull

LONDON

ROUTLEDGE & KEGAN PAUL

First published 1968
by Routledge & Kegan Paul Ltd
Broadway House, 68–74 Carter Lane
London, E.C.4

Printed in Great Britain
by Northumberland Press Limited
Gateshead

© *Arthur Pollard 1968*

SBN 7100 6134 X (C)
SBN 7100 6135 8 (P)

The Profiles in Literature Series

This series is designed to provide the student of literature and the general reader with a brief and helpful introduction to the major novelists and prose writers in English, American and foreign literature.

Each volume will provide an account of an individual author's writing career and works, through a series of carefully chosen extracts illustrating the major aspects of the author's art. These extracts are accompanied by commentary and analysis, drawing attention to particular features of the style and treatment. There is no pretence, of course, that a study of extracts can give a sense of the works as a whole, but this selective approach enables the reader to focus his attention upon specific features, and to be informed in his approach by experienced critics and scholars who are contributing to the series.

The volumes will provide a particularly helpful and practical form of introduction to writers whose works are extensive or which present special problems for the modern reader, who can then proceed with a sense of his bearings and an informed eye for the writer's art.

An important feature of these books is the extensive reference list of the author's works and the descriptive list of the most useful biographies, commentaries and critical studies.

B.C.S.

Contents

CONTENTS

Charlotte Brontë—her life and works

There is a cult of the Brontës, and Mrs. Gaskell was amongst
its earliest devotees. Anne and Emily Brontë were both
dead when she met Charlotte in 1850. She was deeply
moved by the harsh circumstances of Charlotte's life—
alone with an eccentric father in a bleak moorland parsonage, after having had to suffer far more than her fair
share of life's ills. No wonder Mrs. Gaskell could say : 'Such
a life as Miss Brontë's I never heard of before' (*Letters of
Mrs. Gaskell*, ed. J. A. V. Chapple and Arthur Pollard, 1966,
p. 124). Millions have read about that life as Mrs. Gaskell
described it. Haworth has long been a place of pilgrimage.

Family life and friends

The biography, however, merely confirmed what the
novels first stated. Charlotte Brontë turned a lot of her
autobiography into fiction. She wrote four novels—*Jane
Eyre* (1847), *Shirley* (1849), *Villette* (1853) and *The Professor*
(1857). This last, though written first, was published pos-
thumously (she died in 1855 at the age of thirty-eight). The
action of the last two is principally located in Brussels and
no doubt draws largely upon the author's own stay in

that city, both learning and teaching in the school of M. Héger, with whom she fell in love. *Jane Eyre* is even more dependent on its writer's own experiences—Cowan Bridge School was the model for Lowood, and Jane Eyre, like Charlotte Brontë herself, knows the problems and difficulties of life as a governess. Many of the characters in the novels are modelled on people Charlotte knew, and even in the least autobiographical of all the novels, *Shirley*, the heroine was based on Emily Brontë (*Letters of Mrs. Gaskell*, p. 249) and the Yorke family modelled on Charlotte's friends, the Taylors.

It was a narrow life that Charlotte lived. She did not know many people or many places. The story of the Brontës is well-known and needs but brief re-telling. Patrick Brontë was an Irishman, a Protestant Evangelical, who, after short spells as a curate in other areas of Yorkshire, became incumbent of Haworth near Keighley in 1820 (Charlotte was then four years old), where he remained till his death in 1861. There his five daughters and one son grew up and died. The two eldest, Maria and Elizabeth, died in 1825 of disease probably contracted at Cowan Bridge School, to which all the daughters but Anne were sent. Charlotte later went to Miss Wooler's school at Roe Head and taught there from 1835 to 1838. After unpleasant experience as a governess, she went with Emily to Brussels in 1842 where she served as a pupil-teacher in M. Héger's school.

But the sisters were soon back at Haworth, and in the years that followed they wrote the books which have since immortalised them and the place from which they came. Emily's *Wuthering Heights*, a story of Lear-like intensity, is set in the bleak moors near the Brontës' home. Setting matches atmosphere, but the novel's fundamental quality derives from Emily's own character, from her own fearful intensity which was enough to frighten Mrs. Gaskell

2

even at second hand. By contrast, Anne, the youngest sister, seems also to have been the gentlest. Charlotte seems to have had an elasticity of temperament which certainly at times embraced the gentleness of Anne, even if it did not quite reach the fearful intensity of Emily. This in itself may have something to do with her achievement. Lacking Emily's genius, she yet seems to have had a wider sympathy and probably a broader competence. Just as she attained success as a writer, personal calamity descended in the deaths of her dipsomaniac brother, Branwell, and her remaining sisters, Emily and Anne, within a few months of each other in 1848 and 1849. She herself married her father's curate, A. B. Nicholls, in 1854, but died a few months later at the age of thirty-eight.

Romanticism

Within the narrow confines of Haworth parsonage and dependent so much upon themselves, the Brontë children invented a fantasy world about which they wrote at length. To the gift of intense imagination was added the quality of intense passion. The narrowness of Charlotte's experience makes autobiography important in the matter of her novels. Her imagination and passion exalts the subjectivity of her work. In both good ways and bad, she is an example of the extreme Romantic. She expresses, but rarely analyses, feelings. Her characters, and especially her heroines, are often isolated, often oppressed, often introspective. Thus there is plenty of pining, abundance of wishful anticipation, enough of sentimentalism and a fair proportion of melodrama. In this respect she demonstrates latter-day Gothic at times.

This was all part of her urge to break out (cf. the dialogue between Rose and Caroline sparked off by Mrs. Radcliffe's *The Italian—Shirley*, ch. 23). That breaking out demanded a fantasy-ending different from the drab life she led, and, with the exception of *Villette*, and even that is clothed in ambiguity, the novels end happily. After hopeless yearning Cinderella gains her prince, but in this case, by contrast with the fairy tales, against the added odds that it is Cinderella who is plain and her rivals who are beautiful. Here is yet another autobiographical influence—Charlotte considered herself plain. The endings are, however, acceptable because they form part of an integrated whole. The same applies to some of the more exaggerated episodes. There is nothing synthetic about the exaggeration. Charlotte Brontë's imagination constantly magnifies her experience, and this makes her a disturbing writer at times.

Style

Two devices in particular (if one may call them such) Charlotte Brontë adopts for relating the world of her novels to our world. One is the autobiographical method of narration, whereby the main character tells his or her own story. The authorial 'I' always represents a large claim for credibility, and in Charlotte Brontë's case, because there is much in the heroine's history that duplicate's the novelist's own, this claim is strengthened yet more. The second device (and it is here where I am most doubtful about the use of this word) for relating the world of the novel is that of the dominant point of view. Lucy Snowe and Jane Eyre, the latter especially, are not only, in large part, biographical synonyms for Charlotte Brontë; they are also her moral *alter egos*. Lord David Cecil has called her 'a Puritan moralist' (*Early Victorian Novelists*, 1960 edn., p. 127), and this is true enough. Her heroines at times can be upright almost to the point of priggishness. The important thing in the present context, however. is to stress that this moralism

4

represents a stabilising factor, countering some of the exaggerations already referred to.

Charlotte Brontë's superiority to the Gothic, however, is more than an added infusion of moralism. The poet Crabbe has more than once succinctly characterised the Gothic mode, of which the following is but a brief example:

> She likes to read of strange and bold escapes,
> Of plans and plottings, murders and mishaps,
> Love in all hearts, and lovers in all shapes.
> *Posthumous Tales*, XV, 'Belinda Waters',
> II, 50–52

Charlotte Brontë's novels are both more and less than this. There is no 'thriller' element for its own sake. The ingredients may not be very much different from the Gothic —fire, storm, madness, apparitions—and the description is sometimes evidently heightened, but choice of incident and manner of description are always made to serve the overall purpose of demonstrating a view of life. Events affect character, and character reacts to events. Charlotte Brontë transcends the Gothic by her revelation of the ways in which the characters respond. The reader senses the pressures of life, as human resilience resists and modifies the situation with which it is confronted. It is here, of course, that the Puritan strain becomes important, for Charlotte Brontë's moralism interacts with her romanticism. This moralism helps us to accept the sometimes rather stark and unsubtle black-and-white contrast of good and evil. We believe in her good and evil because she believes in them; that is, though we might not accept such simplicities in isolation, we are prepared to accept them in the context in which Charlotte Brontë asks us to do so. This is another way in which her subjectivism operates. Her own feelings, her own attitudes, her own experience—these, far more than in most writers, form the staple of her work.

Strong passions, stern morals, hard life—these are the real stuff of the novels. The happy endings are there, but these are not just the wish-fulfilment that some critics have considered them to be. Like the suffering that precedes them, they are the product of Charlotte Brontë's Romantic intensity. This intensity never reached the tragic grandeur of Emily's solitary novel, and this may explain why Charlotte's is often considered the secondary talent. We need, however, to remember the greater variety of her work and the extraordinary achievement in some episodes and phases. Nowhere is this better shown than in *Jane Eyre*, and especially in the Lowood chapters of that novel. It is at once clearer, simpler and yet more intense than the other works. That is why it is the most memorable. Like all her novels, but best of all, it shows Charlotte Brontë's view of life, in Lord David Cecil's phrase, 'not as a garden of pleasure, but as a tense and sublime battle' (*op. cit.*, p. 133). Life as a tense and sublime battle is surely one of the eternal verities. The measure of her success in representing it is the measure of Charlotte Brontë's claim to immortality.

Scheme of extracts

Charlotte Brontë's main interest lies in the history of her heroines. There is therefore a central section on these characters, but in order to appreciate their place in the novels properly, this section is preceded by two others dealing with events and with other characters. There is also a preliminary section without extracts, giving the briefest necessary account of the novels' outlines and structure. Later sections deal with the handling of time and place, speech and dialogue, and the author's place in the novels. By this arrangement it is hoped that the particularity of Charlotte Brontë's approach to the novel will appear. Some idea of the differing treatment accorded to and success achieved by her various characters should emerge, and there should also be some indication of the recurrent themes and attitudes mentioned in the introductory pages above.

Outline and structure

It may be useful to begin with a brief outline of the story in Charlotte Brontë's four novels. The first and the last, *The Professor* and *Villette*, are set chiefly in Brussels. Their main characters are both teachers, Crimsworth in the former and Lucy Snowe in the latter novel. Both are concerned with characters isolated in a strange environment and both show the development of a love-interest, in Crimsworth's case ending happily, in Lucy's much more doubtfully. This difference marks a contrast between the two novels; Lucy's course is always much more stormy, much less predictable than that of her male counterpart. *Villette* is, psychologically speaking, altogether a richer novel than its predecessor. The vicissitudes of the isolated heroine were first traced in *Jane Eyre*, in which the principal character tells her life-story over its most important period stretching from the sojourn as an orphan in the home of an unsympathetic aunt through cruel schooldays and a tumultuous period of suffering ending in her marriage to Rochester in whose house she had exercised her care as governess to his ward. Much of her suffering stems from her relationship with Rochester, just as much of Lucy Snowe's derives from the behaviour of Monsieur Paul Emanuel. Both men are dominating and even domineering figures. *Shirley*, by contrast, takes its title from its central dominating female character. It is the only one of the novels narrated in the third person. More like Emily than herself, Charlotte perhaps did not trust herself to let Shirley tell her own tale. In any case, the structure and the time of this novel are different. It is historical, set in the time of the Luddite Riots of 1812. It covers a broader field, taking in not only the personal relationships of Shirley but also those of the more retiring Caroline Helstone, and, in addition, concerning itself extensively with the public topic of industrial unrest and with the tracing of relationships within the neighbourhood as a whole.

Against this brief summary we may now turn to an examination of the manner in which Charlotte Brontë constructed her novels. Taking them in order of composition, we will consider first *The Professor*. Like *Jane Eyre* and *Villette*, it is told in the narrator-hero(ine)'s first person, but by contrast with these two novels it covers a lesser span of time. There is little reference to William Crimsworth's childhood, and what there is, is retrospective and reported, not immediate and dramatised. In fact, Crimsworth's life up to the beginning of the events in the novel is covered quickly and rather crudely by the artificial device of 'a letter, sent by me a year since to an old school acquaintance' (of whom we hear no more) which occupies most of the first chapter. Thereafter the novel is worked out in two locations, first in Yorkshire covering Crimsworth's employment and ultimate break with his manufacturer-brother, and then in Brussels, where Crimsworth gains employment as a schoolmaster. There the interest divides between the passion of Mlle. Zoraïde Reuter for him (and the consequent jealousy of M. Pelet, her lover whom she eventually marries) and his own for Mlle. Frances Henri, whom he himself marries. One other character

CB—B   9 should be mentioned, the blunt, outspoken Yorke Hunsden, whom Crimsworth meets in Yorkshire and who conveniently turns up at the critical period in Brussels so as to act as confidant, commentator and chorus at several points in the novel. There is much in this book that, *mutatis mutandis*, resembles *Villette*, and this is not surprising, for Charlotte's husband, A. B. Nicholls, in his preface to *The Professor*, records that 'Being dissuaded from her intention [of publishing *The Professor*], the authoress made some use of the materials in a subsequent work—*Villette*'. This early novel, however, lacks the variety and sustained interest of its successor.

Jane Eyre covers a much greater stretch of time. Its outline is clearly divisible into the three sections covering Jane's sojourns first at Lowood School, then with Rochester at Thornfield Hall, and finally with the Rivers at Moor House. The initial portrayal of Jane as the oppressed child establishes a much stronger sense of emotional participation in the reader than is ever the case in *The Professor*. Two things may be noted here—first, that we have a child in the one novel, and an adult in the other; second, that we have in the one a girl, in the other a man. Age and sex both operate in favour of sympathy for Jane. She is also an orphan, and to the sympathy inevitable for her state, is added that for the way in which she is treated. The first part of *Jane Eyre* is thus devoted to the establishment of a tremendous sense of emotional identification with the heroine. The second part extends and subtilises this whilst at the same time broadening the narrative interest of the novel. Jane's interest in Rochester means that he comes to dominate it. Who is he? What is his history? Will he marry Blanche Ingram? These are some of the questions raised against the background of events as various as the mysterious noises, the house-party, the 'gipsy' episode and ultimately Rochester's proposal and his attempted bigamy.

This last marks a climax in the action. Jane escapes, and in the last part we find a new interest, her accession to wealth and her discovery of her relationship with the Rivers, her resistance to St. John's proposals and her eventual 'supernatural' recall to Rochester.

Villette can be taken next, though out of chronological order, as the third and last of the autobiographical novels. The title itself is significant, referring not as in the other two novels to the principal character but to the place in which most of the action takes place. In this novel Charlotte Brontë has taken a broader canvas; it is not so simply the history of the heroine. This meant that she was faced with a more complicated problem of disposition and arrangement. This was also a problem in *Shirley*. First, one needs to ask whether the introductory chapters needed to take up so much space in giving their account of Lucy Snowe's early years with the Brettons and Miss Marchmont, for the book only really begins in Villette. There Lucy takes a job as a teacher, and against a background of incident which, whilst not extensive, is sufficiently varied, the relationships of the main characters are worked out. The incidents include a play, a concert and a fête (all, be it noted theatrical, divorced from the real world), but more important than any of these are, first, the attitudes the characters display on these occasions and, secondly, events which serve primarily, if not exclusively, to bring out characters' feelings such as Lucy's 'confession' to the priest. Basically, four characters matter, namely, Lucy herself, the scintillating Ginevra Fanshawe, Dr. John Bretton and Monsieur Paul Emanuel, but by contrast with *The Professor* and *Jane Eyre* there are more, and more substantial secondary characters to provide depth. Bretton's attraction to the fascinating but worthless Ginevra is considered at length, but the fact that it has to be shown mainly from Lucy's angle makes it lose some of its possible force. This is emphasised by the unbalance between the tracing of this relationship and of those of Lucy herself, and especially of that between Lucy and M. Paul. Both Dr. John and Ginevra are required as foils for Lucy in the first half of the novel, Ginevra for her beauty and success in affairs of the heart, Dr. John for his attractiveness and thereby his contrast to the man whom Lucy will eventually love. The novel develops in intensity as M. Paul comes to the fore, and Charlotte Brontë makes much of the stress between his love and his faith (the latter in many ways personified in the somewhat sinister Madame Beck). The developing, deepening affection of M. Paul, often expressed in outbursts of jealousy, is one of Charlotte Brontë's major successes in character-portrayal, not least because it has to be expressed through the mouth of that love's object and that jealousy's victim, Lucy herself.

Shirley is the only one of the novels omnisciently narrated in the third person. It also takes the broadest canvas. In fact, it represents the panorama of a community. It is also historical. In some ways the extent of her task seems to have proved difficult for Charlotte Brontë. The book reveals problems of organisation. It begins with a meeting of the three curates, whose appearances, dispersed and mainly in the first part, provide occasion for comedy and satire. It moves next to the subject of Robert Moore's new textile machinery, and this topic, and especially opposition to its introduction, provides recurring interest with influence upon the personal relationships within the novel. The third chapter presents the Yorke family who re-appear periodically, but who nevertheless remain at all times subsidiary. It is not until the sixth chapter that any prominence is given to Caroline Helstone, whose love for Robert is one of the major themes of the book, whilst we must wait patiently until the eleventh chapter before the heroine, Shirley Keeldar, makes her appearance. Thereafter Charlotte

Brontë traced interesting affinities and differences between these two main characters, but we still have to wait until the final third of the book before the question of Shirley's marriage is presented with much sense of urgency, and even then the critical event, the interview between herself and Louis Moore, is presented at one remove, and that the altogether unconvincing device of Louis's recording this interview in his note-book. The novel does not hold its various interests in equipoise, but rather seems to sway from one area of interest to another, almost at times to the oblivion of the topics not under consideration. Charlotte Brontë's return to the autobiographical method of narration and to a narrower canvas in her last novel *Villette* may well have owed something to her experience in *Shirley*.

Her novels can hardly be said to be well constructed. There are too many loose ends. There are also too many resorts to the unlikely and the melodramatic, such as, for instance, Caroline's discovery of Mrs. Pryor as her long-lost mother. There is also unevenness of pace, especially when the work is held up for discussion of subjects which have at best only peripheral relevance to the work as a whole (cf. *Shirley*, ch. 23). What they lack in art, however, they make up in authenticity. Their emotional strength and sincerity ensures that the reader goes on.

Events

A novel is the total impression created by a series of related events. Though Charlotte Brontë is very subjective in her approach and concerned largely with character, it is through events as much as dialogue, description or any-else that we gain our view of her characters. We need therefore to examine her description of important events.

Here is her account of William Crimsworth's finding his pupil Frances who had silently disappeared and for whom he had sought diligently. He is wandering in the Protestant cemetery at Louvain and finds her by her mother's grave.

I

Importuned by the sound of my own footsteps, I turned off upon the turf, and slowly advanced to a grove of yews; I saw something stir among the stems; I thought it might be a broken branch swinging, my short-sighted vision had caught no form, only a sense of motion; but the dusky shade passed on, appearing and disappearing at the openings in the avenue. I soon discerned it was a living thing, and a human thing; and, drawing nearer, I perceived it was a woman, pacing slowly to and fro, and evidently deeming herself alone as I had deemed myself alone, and meditating as I had been meditating. Ere long she returned to a seat which I fancy she had just quitted, or I should have caught sight of her before. It was in a nook, screened by a clump of trees; there was the white wall before her, and a little stone set up against the wall, and at the foot of the stone was an allotment of turf freshly turned up, a new-made grave. I put on my spectacles, and passed softly close behind her; glancing at the inscription on the stone, I read, 'Julienne Henri, died at Brussels, aged sixty. August 10th, 18—.' Having perused the inscription, I looked down at the form sitting bent and thoughtful just under my eyes, unconscious of the vicinity of any living thing; it was a slim, youthful figure in mourning apparel of the plainest black stuff, with a little, simple, black crape bonnet; I felt, as well as saw, who it was; and, moving neither hand nor foot, I stood for some moments enjoying the security of conviction. I had sought her for a month, and had never discovered one of her traces—never met a hope, or seized a chance of encountering her anywhere. I had been forced to loosen my grasp on expectation; and, but an hour ago, had sunk slackly under the discouraging thought that the current of life, and the impulse of destiny, had swept her for ever from my reach; and, behold, while bending suddenly earthward beneath the pressure of despondency—while following with my eyes the track of sorrow on the turf of a graveyard—here was my lost jewel dropped on the tear-fed herbage, nestling in the mossy and mouldy roots of yew-trees.

Frances sat very quiet, her elbow on her knee, and her head on her hand. I knew she could retain a thinking attitude a long time without change; at last, a tear fell; she had been looking at the name on the stone before her, and her heart had no doubt endured one of those constrictions with which the desolate living, regretting the dead, are, at times, so sorely oppressed. Many tears rolled down, which she wiped away, again and again, with her handkerchief; some distressed sobs escaped her, and then, the paroxysm over, she sat quiet as before. I put my hand gently on her shoulder; no need further to prepare her, for she was neither hysterical nor liable to fainting-fits; a sudden push, indeed, might have startled her, but the contact of my quiet touch merely woke attention as I wished; and though she turned quickly, yet so lightning-swift is thought—in some minds especially—I believe the wonder of what—the conscious-ness of who it was that thus stole unawares on her solitude, had passed through her brain, and flashed into her heart, even before she had effected that hasty movement; at least, Amazement had hardly opened her eyes and raised them to mine, ere Recognition informed their irids with most speak-ing brightness. Nervous surprise had hardly discomposed her features ere a sentiment of most vivid joy shone clear and warm on her whole countenance. I had hardly time to observe that she was wasted and pale, ere called to feel a responsive inward pleasure by the sense of most full and exquisite pleasure glowing in the animated flush, and shin-ing in the expansive light, now diffused over my pupil's face. It was the summer sun flashing out after the heavy summer shower; and what fertilises more rapidly than that beam, burning almost like fire in its ardour?

I hate boldness—that boldness which is of the brassy brow and insensate nerves; but I love the courage of the strong heart, the fervour of the generous blood; I loved with passion the light of Frances Evans' clear hazel eye when it did not fear to look straight into mine; I loved the tones with which she uttered the words—

'Mon maître! mon maître!'

The Professor, ch. 19

This passage begins with two characters isolated from each other. This is brought out by the reference to Frances's 'deeming herself alone as I had deemed myself alone, and meditating as I had been meditating'. The setting is appro-priate—a graveyard. The passage preceding that quoted above describes the scene. This one begins with the relation-ship of character to place. The very first word makes this clear. 'Importuned' draws our attention to Crimsworth's feelings. There then follows the gradual recognition; notice 'a living thing . . . a human thing . . . a woman'. Before the precise recognition takes place, there is the pause to describe the tomb by which she sits. This also, however, is a step in the reader's process of recognition : if anything, confirming what he must already have suspected. Then Crimsworth himself completes his process of recognition —in a sentence that combines power with simplicity : 'I *felt*, as well as saw, who it was.' This simplicity is part of the broad effect of the scene. The description of the place does not carry much detail, and the girl herself is almost starkly presented—'a slim, youthful figure in mourning apparel of the plainest black stuff, with a little, simple, black crape bonnet'.

By contrast with this we notice the abstraction—'enjoying the security of the conviction'. This is the preface to Crimsworth's brief descent into reminiscence, recalling the hopelessness of the month past. A whole series of phrases reinforce this idea—'loosen my grasp', 'sunk slackly', 'discouraging thought', 'bending . . . beneath the pressure of despondency', all to be contrasted with the vivid image that ends the paragraph. The image might indeed seem too poetic; 'tear-fed herbages' seems very self-conscious. There is even a hint of the grotesque. Frances may be his 'lost jewel', but 'nesting in . . . mouldy roots' appears hardly appropriate.

The graveyard, however, place of sadness, has become by happy irony the scene of renewed joy and life. That life is not yet evident in Frances herself. She more appropriately to the place is statuesque, but also weeping. Her stillness is broken by a paroxysm of grief. There follows the most significant event in the whole incident—again simple and quiet—'I put my hand gently on her shoulder'. Charlotte Brontë then gets the sense of disturbance that is contemporary with, perhaps even precedes, the full realisation of

17

recognition, through the broken syntax of the following sentence. Then another change of style—into the use of formal personifications 'Amazement' and 'Recognition', this too distancing the thing, giving a sense of something other than self. And the next sentence too has abstract subjects. We are coming slowly to Frances herself in such a phrase as 'discomposed her features', and only later do we reach 'animated flush' and 'expansive light'. Again the paragraph ends with a formal image, but there is now an added rhetorical question. This reminds us that Crimsworth is telling us about it all. One wonders whether greater immediacy might have resulted if Frances could have been more directly involved (see the next extract). What does result, however, is an especial power in her outburst at the climax of the scene.

In the next passage we read of Jane Eyre's return to Rochester (they had parted after their marriage-ceremony was stopped by the revelation that Rochester's first wife, a mad woman, was still alive and confined at Thornfield Hall).

2

I proceeded: at last my way opened, the trees thinned a little; presently I beheld a railing, then the house—scarce, by this dim light, distinguishable from the trees; so dank and green were its decaying walls. Entering a portal, fastened only by a latch, I stood amidst a space of enclosed ground, from which the wood swept away in a semicircle. There were no flowers, no garden-beds; only a broad gravel walk girdling a grass plot, and this set in the heavy frame of the forest. The house presented two pointed gables in its front; the windows were latticed and narrow, the front door was narrow too, one step led up to it. The whole looked, as the host of the Rochester Arms had said, 'quite a desolate spot'. It was as still as a church on a week-day:

the pattering rain on the forest leaves was the only sound audible in its vicinage.

'Can there be life here?' I asked.

Yes, life of some kind there was; for I heard movement —that narrow front door was unclosing, and some shape was about to issue from the grange.

It opened slowly: a figure came out into the twilight and stood on the step—a man without a hat. He stretched forth his hand as if to feel whether it rained. Dusk as it was, I recognised him; it was my master, Edward Fairfax Rochester, and no other.

I stayed my step, almost my breath, and stood to watch him—to examine him, myself unseen, and alas! to him invisible. It was a sudden meeting, and one in which rapture was kept well in check by pain. I had no difficulty in restraining my voice from exclamation, my step from hasty advance.

His form was of the same strong and stalwart contour as ever: his port was still erect, his hair was still raven black: nor were his features altered or sunk: not in one year's space, by any sorrow, could his athletic strength be quelled or his vigorous prime blighted. But in his countenance I saw a change: that looked desperate and brooding—that reminded me of some wronged and fettered wild beast or bird, dangerous to approach in his sullen woe. The caged eagle, whose gold-ringed eyes cruelty has extinguished, might look as looked that sightless Samson.

And reader, do you think I feared him in his blind ferocity?—if you do, you little know me. A soft hope blent with my sorrow that soon I should dare to drop a kiss on that brow of rock, and on those lips so sternly sealed beneath it; but not yet. I would not accost him yet.

He descended the one step, and advanced slowly and gropingly towards the grass plot. Where was his daring stride now? Then he paused, as if he knew not which way to turn. He lifted his hand and opened his eyelids; gazed blank, and with a straining effort, on the sky, and toward the amphitheatre of trees: one saw that all to him was void darkness. He stretched his right hand (the left arm, the mutilated one, he kept hidden in his bosom); he seemed to wish by touch to gain an idea of what lay around him : he met but vacancy still; for the trees were some yards off where he stood. He relinquished the endeavour, folded his arms, and stood quiet and mute in the rain, now falling fast on his uncovered head.

(Jane speaks to the servants and then goes into the parlour where Rochester has already gone.)

'Give the tray to me; I will carry it in.'

I took it from her hand : she pointed me out the parlour door. The tray shook as I held it; the water spilt from the glass; my heart struck my ribs loud and fast. Mary opened the door for me, and shut it behind me.

This parlour looked gloomy : a neglected handful of fire burnt low in the grate; and, leaning over it, with his head supported against the high, old-fashioned mantelpiece, appeared the blind tenant of the room. His old dog, Pilot, lay on one side, removed out of the way, and coiled up as if afraid of being inadvertently trodden upon. Pilot pricked up his ears when I came in : then he jumped up with a yelp and a whine, and bounded towards me : he almost knocked the tray from my hands. I set it on the table; then patted him, and said softly, 'Lie down!' Mr. Rochester turned mechanically to *see* what the commotion was : but as he *saw* nothing, he returned and sighed.

'Give me the water, Mary,' he said.

I approached him with the now only half-filled glass; Pilot followed me, still excited.

'What is the matter?' he inquired.

'Down, Pilot!' I again said. He checked the water on its way to his lips, and seemed to listen : he drank, and put the glass down. 'This is you, Mary, is it not?'

'Mary is in the kitchen,' I answered.

He put out his hand with a quick gesture, but not seeing where I stood, he did not touch me. 'Who is this? Who is
20

this?' he demanded, trying, as it seemed, to *see* with those sightless eyes—unavailing and distressing attempt! 'Answer me—speak again!' he ordered, imperiously and aloud.

'Will you have a little more water, sir? I spilt half of what was in the glass,' I said.

'*Who* is it? *What* is it? Who speaks?'

'Pilot knows me, and John and Mary know I am here. I came only this evening,' I answered.

'Great God!—what delusion has come over me? What sweet madness has seized me?'

'No delusion—no madness: your mind, sir, is too strong for delusions, your health too sound for frenzy.'

'And where is the speaker? Is it only a voice? Oh I *cannot* see, but I must feel, or my heart will stop and my brain burst. Whatever, whoever you are, be perceptible to the touch, or I cannot live!'

He groped; I arrested his wandering hand, and prisoned it in both mine.

'Her very fingers!' he cried; 'her small, slight fingers! If so, there must be more of her.'

The muscular hand broke from my custody; my arm was seized, my shoulder, neck, waist—I was entwined and gathered to him.

'Is it Jane? *What* is it? This is her shape—this is her size—'

'And this her voice,' I added. 'She is all here: her heart, too. God bless you, sir! I am glad to be so near you again.'

'Jane Eyre!—Jane Eyre!' was all he said.

Jane Eyre, ch. 37

This also is a recognition scene, but in striking contrast to the previous extract. They compare in their initial evocation of the scene, but even here the differences are quickly apparent. This passage is more precise, more detailed. Even the negatives give a sense of detail—'no flowers, no garden-beds'. There is a sense of much greater vitality than in the passage from *The Professor*, and as a result a sense of more powerful, if for the greater part suppressed, passion. This can be noted in the heroine's self-questioning. The drama of this is reinforced by the answer, where again there is contrast with *The Professor*. Whereas there Frances is still and quiet, here there is movement, an entry. Every word tells in the simple description—'A figure came out into the twilight and stood on the step—a man with a hat.' The dramatic quality is enhanced not only by the recognition, but by the very personal terms in which Jane states it—'*my* master, Edward Fairfax Rochester'. There follows the terse description of her own tense condition.

The next phase in the passage gives us Jane's more considered contemplation of him. There are the ways in which he is the same and those in which he has changed. She chooses, however, not to lay principal stress upon his physical change, his blindness, but rather upon what the physical reveals of a deeper change that made him look 'desperate and brooding'. There follows another of Charlotte Brontë's formal similes, but this time it seems more integrated and more powerful than those in the previous extract. It is altogether appropriate to conceive of Rochester as a 'caged eagle' and 'sightless Samson'. Indeed, this latter image has more than the associations of blindness and strength; it reminds us that Rochester, like Samson, had suffered through infatuation for an unworthy woman. The whole of this phase maintains a balanced interplay between what Rochester looked like (and often implicitly what he must have been feeling) and what Jane felt about him. Charlotte Brontë heightens this sense of Jane's feelings by the introduction of the sudden intimacy when Jane turns to the reader to ask, 'Do you think I feared him in his blind ferocity?'

The second half of this extract brings the two characters into close contact. It is so arranged as to endow a commonplace incident with considerable potentiality for surprise.

It begins with Jane's own feelings of agitation, again so simply expressed—'my heart struck my ribs loud and fast'. The dog is made to play a key role, and ironically he can recognise where his master cannot, a point that Charlotte Brontë emphasises by her references in words which she herself italicises to Rochester's turning 'to *see* . . . but he *saw* nothing'. As a result, the dialogue takes on an especial urgency and importance, especially in Rochester's questions. The whole passage then, both in speech and action, steadily rises to the crescendo of the final utterly simple exclamation. Here too the contrast with *The Professor* is so marked in its vitality, activity and sheer physical passion.

Something of the extent of Charlotte Brontë's emotional range may be gathered from a comparison of this passage with two others. The first describes a cry in the night (actually that of the mad woman who has not, however, at this stage been identified as Mrs. Rochester).

3

I had forgotten to draw my curtain, which I usually did, and also to let down my window-blind. The consequence was, that when the moon, which was full and bright (for the night was fine), came in her course to that space in the sky opposite my casement, and looked in at me through the unveiled panes, her glorious gaze roused me. Awakening in the dead of night, I opened my eyes on her disc— silver-white and crystal clear. It was beautiful, but too solemn : I half rose, and stretched my arm to draw the curtain.

Good God! What a cry!

The night—its silence—its rest, was rent in twain by a savage, a sharp, a shrilly sound that ran from end to end of Thornfield Hall.

My pulse stopped : my heart stood still; my stretched arm was paralysed. The cry died, and was not renewed.

Indeed, whatever being uttered that fearful shriek could not soon repeat it: not the wildest-winged condor on the Andes could, twice in succession, send out such a yell from the cloud shrouding his eyrie. The thing delivering such utterance must rest ere it could repeat the effort.

It came out of the third story; for it passed overhead. And overhead—yes, in the room just above my chamber-ceiling —I now heard a struggle: a deadly one it seemed from the noise; and a half-smothered voice shouted—

'Help! Help! Help!' three times rapidly.

'Will no one come?' it cried; and then, while the staggering and stamping went on wildly, I distinguished through plank and plaster:

'Rochester! Rochester! for God's sake, come!'

A chamber-door opened: some one ran, or rushed, along the gallery. Another step stamped on the flooring above and something fell: and there was silence.

Jane Eyre, ch. 20

This passage begins with a heightened, poetic description. The moonlight shining into the bedroom provides a conventional but none the less vivid scene. 'Silver-white and crystal clear' emphasise the beauty, but Charlotte Brontë goes on to say it was 'too solemn'. This introduces Jane's feelings. There is just a hint of foreboding, but before we can fully appreciate this we are electrified, as Jane was, by an exclamation. She had heard Mrs. Rochester's cry; we read of her reaction to it, startled and fearful. She then describes it, first by recalling us to the 'silence' and 'rest' of the night that preceded the cry, and then by emphasising the horror of the cry, singling out its qualities by isolating the adjectives after the repeated indefinite article. After the instinctive reaction ('Good God! What a cry!') we have the description of physical response ('My pulse stopped', etc.). We have, that is, the immediate dramatic response and then the account of consequent condition. Jane then thinks of the cry itself and Charlotte Brontë again has recourse to reference to birds of prey. The account then returns to what is happening, but it is at a distance—necessary action, increasing the mystery but not the horror, for nothing could add to that first frightful cry. The passage ends in mystery—'*something* fell, and there was silence'.

In the second of these two extracts to show Charlotte Brontë's emotional range further Jane Eyre, having left Rochester after the attempted bigamy, comes exhausted at the end of her wanderings to a lonely house. The 'honest but inflexible servant' rebuffs her plea for shelter.

4

This was the climax. A pang of exquisite suffering—a throe of true despair—rent and heaved my heart. Worn out, indeed, I was; not another step could I stir. I sank on the wet doorstep; I groaned—I wrung my hands—I wept in utter anguish. Oh, this spectre of death! Oh, this last hour, approaching in such horror! Alas, this isolation—this banishment from my kind! Not only the anchor of hope, but the footing of fortitude was gone—at least for a moment; but the last I soon endeavoured to regain.

'I can but die,' I said, 'and I believe in God. Let me try to wait His will in silence.'

Jane Eyre, ch. 28

The sentence-structure here is utterly simple: it begins 'This was the climax'. And yet this structure is also varied to get the right emphasis. There is the degree of exclamation that we might expect from a description of such circumstances as the passage is concerned with. There is some parallelism, but there is also effective variation through the use of inversion, for instance ('Worn out, indeed, I was'). There is also a careful progression from this physical suffering through to the mental distress ('this spectre of death . . . this isolation'). Then the language changes to that almost of the pulpit ('anchor of hope', footing of fortitude') with its figurativeness and its abstractions. This is the transitional phase from suffering to determination, so that, whereas the inversion quoted above stresses the first words of physical suffering ('Worn out'), that which closes the paragraph emphasises the last phrase and the new mood ('endeavoured to regain'). Recovered, Jane can now speak in her own person. Charlotte Brontë cleverly abstained from any self-dramatisation by Jane in the earlier mood. The danger of sentimentalising was much too close. When Jane speaks, it is an expression of fortitude and, characteristically, of faith.

Here is a passage from *Villette* describing Lucy Snowe, the heroine of that book, in a somewhat similar condition.

5

If the storm had lulled a little at sunset, it made up now for lost time. Strong and horizontal thundered the current of the wind from north-west to south-east; it brought rain like spray, and sometimes a sharp, hail-like shot; it was cold and pierced me to the vitals. I bent my head to meet it, but it beat me back. My heart did not fail at all in this conflict; I only wished that I had wings and could ascend the gale, spread and repose my pinions on its strength, career in its course, sweep where it swept. While wishing this, I suddenly felt colder where before I was cold, and more powerless where before I was weak. I tried to reach the porch of a great building near, but the mass of frontage and the giant-spire turned black and vanished from my eyes. Instead of sinking on the steps as I intended, I seemed to pitch headlong down an abyss. I remember no more.

Villette, ch. 15

The style of this passage is markedly different from that

in the preceding extract from *Jane Eyre*. There the effect is much more staccato, corresponding to Jane's prolonged, even if not over-long, awareness of her being at the point of collapse. In this passage Lucy is in full control up to the very moment at which she ceases to be in control at all. This gives power to the suddenness and finality of the climax—'I seemed to pitch headlong down an abyss. I remember no more.' This passage also shows devices and usages which, even from the few extracts already quoted, are recognisable as characteristic of their author. One such is the use she makes of the weather, and another is the image once more of the bird of power and strength. Here, however, the image is not so obtrusive as in previous examples.

Lucy teaches in Madame Beck's school, and throughout *Villette* the school and its gardens are visited mysteriously at night by a nun, whether actual or an apparition is for long not clear. Here is one of the appearances:

6

I stood about three yards from a tall, sable-robed, snowy-veiled woman.

Five minutes passed. I neither fled nor shrieked. She was there still. I spoke.

'Who are you? and why do you come to me?'

She stood mute. She had no face—no features: all below her brow was masked with a white cloth; but she had eyes, and they viewed me.

I felt, if not brave, yet a little desperate; and desperation will often suffice to fill the post and do the work of courage. I advanced one step. I stretched out my hand, for I meant to touch her. She seemed to recede. I drew nearer: her recession, still silent, became swift. A mass of shrubs, full-leaved evergreens, laurel and dense yew, intervened between me and what I followed. Having passed that obstacle, I looked and saw nothing. I waited. I said—'If you have any

27

errand to men, come back and deliver it.' Nothing spoke or reappeared.

Villette, ch. 26

and here is the last appearance:

7

Throughout the dormitory, throughout the house, there reigned at this hour the stillness of death. All slept, and in such hush, it seemed that none dreamed. Stretched on the nineteen beds lay nineteen forms, at full length and motionless. On mine—the twentieth couch—nothing *ought* to have lain: I had left it void, and void should have found it. What, then, do I see between the half-drawn curtains? What dark, usurping shape, supine, long, and strange? Is it a robber who has made his way through the open street door, and lies there in wait? It looks very black, I think it looks—not human. Can it be a wandering dog that has come in from the street and crept and nestled hither? Will it spring, will it leap out if I approach? Approach I must. Courage! One step!—

My head reeled, for by the faint night-lamp I saw stretched on my bed the old phantom—the NUN.

A cry at this moment might have ruined me. Be the spectacle what it might, I could afford neither consternation, scream, nor swoon. Besides, I was not overcome. Tempered by late incidents, my nerves disdained hysteria. Warm from illuminations, and music, and thronging thousands, thoroughly lashed up by a new scourge, I defied spectra. In a moment, without exclamation, I had rushed on the haunted couch; nothing leaped out, or sprung, or stirred; all the movement was mine, so was all the life, the reality, the substance, the force; as my instinct felt. I tore her up—the incubus! I held her on high—the goblin! I shook her loose—the mystery! And down she fell—down all around me—down in shreds and fragments—and I trod upon her.

Here again—behold the branchless tree, the unstable

Rosinante; the film of cloud, the flicker of moonshine. The long nun proved a long bolster dressed in a long black stole, and artfully invested with a white veil. The garments in very truth, strange as it may seem, were genuine nun's garments, and by some hand they had been disposed with a view to illusion. Whence came these vestments? Who contrived this artifice? These questions still remained. To the head bandage was pinned a slip of paper: it bore in pencil these mocking words:

'The nun of the attic bequeaths to Lucy Snowe her wardrobe. She will be seen in the Rue Fossette no more.'

Villette, ch. 39

It turns out that the 'nun' has been the disguised lover of one of the girls (cf. Rochester as the 'gypsy' in *Jane Eyre*).

'If not brave, yet a little desperate' is perhaps the key-phrase of the first passage. Here is the apparition again, mysterious, close at hand, unspeaking, even suggestive of the grotesque—'She had no face—no features . . . but she had eyes'. Then there is also the mysterious disappearance. The second passage conveys a distinctly frightening sense —the quiet; the form on the bed; what is it—a robber, a dog? Notice the effect of the questions. Then Lucy's self-bracing—'Approach I must. Courage! One step!'—the horror of recognition—'the NUN'. Next the resolution of desperation, the attack—and the anti-climax! There is a neat succession of dominant emotions, beginning with curiosity and going on through fear, terror, resolution to the final deflation. The syntactical structure matches this succession—first the questions, then the short expressions of resolution, the more detached statements about self-control, followed by the flurry of the attack in the fast and somewhat broken sentences of the latter half of the third paragraph, and finally the more matter-of-fact manner of the last part.

The passages so far examined have dealt with what may

29

be called personal events, that is, incidents as they affected individuals. *Shirley* as a historical novel provides us with examples of the public event. Here is the account of the rioters' attack on Robert Moore's mill.

8

'Shirley—Shirley, the gates are down! That crash was like the felling of great trees. Now they are pouring through. They will break down the mill-doors as they have broken the gate; what can Robert do against so many? Would to God I were a little nearer him—could hear him speak—could speak to him! With my will—my longing to serve him—I could not be a useless burden in his way; I could be turned to some account.'

'They come on!' cried Shirley. 'How steadily they march in! There is discipline in their ranks—I will not say there is courage: hundreds against tens are no proof of that quality; but' (she dropped her voice) 'there is suffering and desperation enough amongst them—these goads will urge them forwards.'

'Forwards against Robert—and they hate him. Shirley, is there much danger they will win the day?'

'We shall see. Moore and Helstone are of "earth's first blood"—no bunglers—no cravens—'

A crash—smash—shiver—stopped their whispers. A simultaneously-hurled volley of stones had saluted the broad front of the mill, with all its windows; and now every pane of every lattice lay in shattered and pounded fragments. A yell followed this demonstration—a rioters' yell—a North-of-England—a Yorkshire—a West-Riding—a West-Riding-clothing-district-of Yorkshire rioters' yell. You never heard that sound, perhaps, reader? So much the better for your ears—perhaps for your heart; since, if it rends the air in hate to yourself, or to the men or principles you approve, the interests to which you wish well, Wrath wakens to the cry of Hate: the Lion shakes his mane, and rises to the howl of the Hyena: Caste stands up, ireful against Caste; and the indignant, wronged spirit of the Middle Rank bears down in zeal and scorn on the famished and furious mass of the Operative Class. It is difficult to be tolerant—difficult to be just—in such moments.

Caroline rose, Shirley put her arm round her: they stood together as still as the straight stems of two trees. That yell was a long one, and when it ceased, the night was yet full of the swaying and murmuring of a crowd.

'What next!' was the question of the listeners. Nothing came yet. The mill remained mute as a mausoleum.

'He *cannot* be alone,' whispered Caroline.

'I would stake all I have, that he is as little alone as he is alarmed,' responded Shirley.

Shots were discharged by the rioters. Had the defenders waited for this signal? It seemed so. The hitherto inert and passive mill woke: fire flashed from its empty window-frames; a volley of musketry pealed sharp through the Hollow.

'Moore speaks at last!' said Shirley, 'and he seems to have the gift of tongues; that was not a single voice.'

'He has been forbearing; no one can accuse him of rashness,' alleged Caroline: 'their discharge preceded his; they broke his gates and his windows; they fired at his garrison before he repelled them.'

What was going on now? It seemed difficult in the darkness, to distinguish, but something terrible, a still renewing tumult was obvious: fierce attacks, desperate repulses; the mill-yard, the mill itself, was full of battle-movement: there was scarcely any cessation now of the discharge of fire-arms; and there was struggling, rushing, trampling, and shouting between. The aim of the assailants seemed to be to enter the mill, that of the defendants to beat them off. They heard the rebel leader cry, 'To the back, lads!' They heard a voice retort, 'Come round, we will meet you!'

'To the counting-house!' was the order again.

'Welcome!—We shall have you there!' was the response. And accordingly, the fiercest blade that had yet glowed,

31

the loudest rattle that had yet been heard, burst from the counting-house front, when the mass of rioters rushed up to it.

The voice that had spoken was Moore's own voice. They could tell by its tones that his soul was now warm with the conflict: they could guess that the fighting animal was roused in every one of those men there struggling together, and was for the time quite paramount above the rational human being.

Both the girls felt their faces glow and their pulses throb; both knew they would do no good by rushing down into the mêlée; they desired neither to deal nor receive blows; but they could not have run away—Caroline no more than Shirley; they could not have fainted; they could not have taken their eyes from the dim, terrible scene—from the mass of cloud, of smoke—the musket-lightning—for the world.

'How and when would it end?' was the demand throbbing in their throbbing pulses. 'Would a juncture arise in which they could be useful?' was what they waited to see: for, though Shirley put off their too-late arrival with a jest, and was ever ready to satirise her own or any other person's enthusiasm, she would have given a farm of her best land for a chance of rendering good service.

The chance was not vouchsafed her; the looked-for juncture never came; it was not likely. Moore had expected this attack for days, perhaps weeks: he was prepared for it at every point. He had fortified and garrisoned his mill, which in itself was a strong building: he was a cool, brave man; he stood to the defence with unflinching firmness; those who were with him caught his spirit, and copied his demeanour. The rioters had never been so met before. At other mills they had attacked, they had found no resistance; an organised, resolute defence was what they never dreamed of encountering. When their leaders saw the steady fire kept up from the mill, witnessed the composure and determination of its owner, heard themselves coolly defied and invited on to death, and beheld their men falling wounded round them, they felt that nothing was to be done here. In haste, they mustered their forces, drew them away from the building: a roll was called over, in which the men answered to figures instead of names: they dispersed wide over the fields, leaving silence and ruin behind them. The attack, from its commencement to its termination had not occupied an hour.

Shirley, ch. 19

Charlotte Brontë uses two angles for this episode, one of narration, the other of feeling. She herself tells of what is going on, and in doing so conveys extremely well the impression of confusion. Notice, for instance, the questions and the tentative nature of some of the answers—'It seemed so', 'It seemed difficult', etc. Notice, too, the way in which we are aware of the narrator's presence but at a distance. She can afford to talk in abstractions—'Wrath wakens to the cry of Hate', etc. All this heightens the contrast with the voice of feeling, of Shirley and Caroline and more especially of the latter, as, more fearful in nature and more tenderly concerned for Moore, she expresses her anxiety for him and her longing to be with him. We need to be fully aware of this further contrast between Shirley and Caroline. The former acts as commentator, announcing what is happening, whilst the latter all the time is in spirit with Moore, trying to realise and thus express sympathetically his point of view. When he himself eventually speaks, they both cease. The excitement is now conveyed through a description of their feelings—'Both the girls felt their faces glow . . .'. The final paragraph represents a foreshortening, a quick summary of the futile encounter. It has no immediacy; it is in the strict sense historical, a narration entirely in the past tense.

The second example from *Shirley* also describes a physical confrontation, this time of rival religious marchers. The Anglicans are led by the militant parson Helstone.

33

9

Old Helstone moved on. Quickening his step, he marched some yards in advance of his company. He had nearly reached the other sable leaders, when he who appeared to act as the hostile commander-in-chief—a large, greasy man, with black hair combed flat on his forehead—called a halt. The procession paused: he drew forth a hymn-book, gave out a verse, set a tune, and they all struck up the most dolorous of canticles.

Helstone signed to his bands: they clashed out with all the power of brass. He desired them to play 'Rule, Britannia,' and ordered the children to join in vocally, which they did with enthusiastic spirit. The enemy was sung and stormed down; his psalm quelled: as far as noise went, he was conquered.

'Now, follow me!' exclaimed Helstone; 'not at a run, but at a firm, smart pace. Be steady, every child and woman of you:—keep together:—hold on by each other's skirts, if necessary.'

And he strode on with such a determined and deliberate gait, and was, besides, so well seconded by his scholars and teachers—who did exactly as he told them, neither running nor faltering, but marching with cool, solid impetus; the curates, too, being compelled to do the same, as they were between two fires,—Helstone and Miss Keeldar, both of whom watched any deviation with lynx-eyed vigilance, and were ready, the one with his cane, the other with her parasol, to rebuke the slightest breach of orders, the least independent or irregular demonstration,—that the body of Dissenters were first amazed, then alarmed, then borne down and pressed back, and at last forced to turn tail and leave the outlet from Roydlane free. Boultby suffered in the onslaught, but Helstone and Malone, between them, held him up, and brought him through the business, whole in limb, though sorely tried in wind.

The fat Dissenter who had given out the hymn was left sitting in the ditch. He was a spirit-merchant by trade, a leader of the Nonconformists, and, it was said, drank more water in that one afternoon than he had swallowed for a twelvemonth before.

Shirley, ch. 17

This is burlesque, a parody of 'Onward, Christian soldiers', except that this hymn had not been written at that time. It is burlesque also of the North-country tradition of 'walking', that is, of processions of religious witness. It strikes us as most un-Christian, and yet it accurately reflects religious feeling of the time. Charlotte Brontë manages the situation neatly for herself, for she liked Helstone little enough but she liked Dissenters even less. Thus her picture of the latter's leader is quite gross caricature—'a large, greasy man'—and his fate is even more so as he finishes in the ditch. Her lack of respect for him is further suggested by the final reference to his trading in and drinking spirits, hardly consonant with a sect which made so much of abstinence from alcohol. Besides the main clash here portrayed, there is the subsidiary latent conflict between Helstone and Shirley against the curates, who, as the next extract shows, were early established as comic and rather unsympathetic characters. Even an incidental touch such as the reference to Boultby's as 'whole in limb, though sorely tried in wind' sustains the broad comedy of the piece.

Characters

We cannot divorce character from event, but in this section an attempt will be made to look at characters in distinction from the setting or circumstances.

Being so subjective in her work, Charlotte Brontë should not surprise us when we discover that she was said to have based a significant part of her characterisation on people she knew. Canon W. M. Heald wrote to Ellen Nussey about *Shirley* in a letter of 8 January, 1850:

Some of them are good enough to tell and need no Oedipus to solve the riddle. I can tabulate, for instance, the Yorke family for the Taylors, Mr. Moore—Mr. Cartwright, and Mr. Helstone is clearly meant for Mr. Roberson, though the authoress has evidently got her idea of his character through an unfavourable medium.

> *The Brontës: Their Lives, Friendships and Correspondence*, ed. Wise and Symington, 1932, III, 64

C. K. Shorter also identified the three curates as J. B. Grant, headmaster of Haworth Grammar School (Donne), J. W. Smith, curate to Patrick Brontë from 1845 to 1847 (Malone), and J. C. Bradley of Oakworth (Sweeting) (*The*

Brontës: Life and Letters, 1908, II, 56–7). *Shirley* begins with the three quarrelsome curates at dinner. The following is an extract from the first chapter.

10

Mr. Malone, who contrived to secure two glasses of wine, when his brethren contented themselves with one, waxed by degrees hilarious after his fashion; that is, he grew a little insolent, said rude things in a hectoring tune, and laughed clamorously at his own brilliancy.

Each of his companions became in turn his butt. Malone had a stock of jokes at their service, which he was accustomed to serve out regularly on convivial occasions like the present, seldom varying his wit; for which, indeed, there was no necessity, as he never appeared to consider himself monotonous, and did not at all care what others thought. Mr. Donne, he favoured with hints about his extreme meagreness, allusions to his turned-up nose, cutting sarcasms on a certain threadbare chocolate surtout, which that gentleman was accustomed to sport whenever it rained, or seemed likely to rain, and criticisms on a choice set of cockney phrases, and modes of pronunciation, Mr. Donne's own property, and certainly deserving of remark for the elegance and finish they communicated to his style.

Mr. Sweeting was bantered about his stature—he was a little man, a mere boy in height and breadth compared with the athletic Malone—rallied on his musical accomplishments—he played the flute and sang hymns like a seraph (some young ladies of his parish thought), sneered at as 'the lady's pet,' teased about his mamma and sisters; for whom poor Mr. Sweeting had some lingering regard, and of whom he was foolish enough now and then to speak in the presence of the priestly Paddy, from whose anatomy the bowels of natural affection had somehow been omitted. . . .

When Malone's raillery became rather too offensive, which it soon did, they joined in an attempt to turn the tables on him, by asking him how many boys had shouted

'Irish Peter!' after him as he came along the road that day (Malone's name was Peter—the Rev. Peter Augustus Malone); requesting to be informed whether it was the mode in Ireland for clergymen to carry loaded pistols in their pockets, and a shillelagh in their hands, when they made pastoral visits; inquiring the signification of such words as vele, firrum, hellum, storrum (so Mr. Malone invariably pronounced veil, firm, helm, storm), and employing such other methods of retaliation as the innate refinement of their minds suggested.

This, of course, would not do. Malone, being neither good-natured nor phlegmatic, was presently in a towering passion. He vociferated, gesticulated; Donne and Sweeting laughed. He reviled them as Saxons and snobs at the very top pitch of his high Celtic voice; they taunted him with being the native of a conquered land. He menaced rebellion in the name of his 'counthry,' vented bitter hatred against English rule; they spoke of rags, beggary, and pestilence. The little parlour was in an uproar; on whatever terms the curates might part to night, they would be sure to meet the best friends in the world to-morrow morning.

Shirley, ch. I

Charlotte Brontë might have chosen to indicate the characters of the curates by a straightforward description. She might also have used actual speech and dialogue. Instead, however, she gives us a report of the drama, of the episode as it took place. This enables her to abstract and emphasise and more easily to give her own slant upon it. Malone is at the centre of it, and even before we are given any examples of his supposed humour, our attitude towards him has already been directed by reference to his greed over the wine and to the egocentricity of his humour ('hilarious after his own fashion', 'laughed clamorously at his own brilliancy'). Moreover, the question of whether it is really humorous is placed in considerable doubt ('a little insolent', 'rude things in a hectoring tone'). Charlotte

38

Brontë then underlines his egocentricity by saying that he seldom varied his wit 'for which, indeed, there was no necessity, as he never appeared to consider himself monotonous, and did not at all care what others thought'. Notice the ironic force in 'for which, indeed, there was no necessity', a clause which deepens the condemnation by its pretence of approval.

We then receive some examples of this wit, first as it affects Donne and then Sweeting. Its crudity in Donne's case is emphasised by its reference to his appearance, speech and poverty, but we are left with the suggestion that the speech was rightly criticised. Charlotte Brontë says herself, not without a note of sarcasm, that it was 'certainly deserving of remark for . . . elegance and finish'. There is a difference in Malone's treatment of the fellow curates. Donne was 'favoured with hints . . . cutting sarcasms . . . criticisms', whereas Sweeting was 'bantered . . . rallied . . . sneered at . . . teased'. Apart from the third of these, Sweeting would appear to be the better treated, but in fact, the things in him that Malone made sport of were more important than those in Donne, and especially the last, Sweeting's affection for his mother and sisters. This helps to present Sweeting as the most attractive of the three, and this impression is strengthened by the respective responses of Donne and himself. Donne stands upon his dignity with 'a stilted self-complacency, and half-sullen phlegm', but that dignity is 'somewhat rickety' anyway, whereas Sweeting reacts with 'the indifference of a light, easy disposition'. There may even be some slight effect in the names, or at any rate in that of Sweeting.

Charlotte Brontë seems to mark the greater enormity of Malone's criticism of Sweeting by a deepening of the satire against the Irishman, who is now described as 'the priestly Paddy, from whose anatomy the bowels of natural affection had somehow been omitted'. The nickname 'priestly

39

Paddy' is turning the scales on Malone by the use of a form of humour apparently as crude as his own. Because she herself has turned upon him, we are all the more on the side of Donne and Sweeting when they do precisely the same thing. The difference in the reaction is, of course, the main point of this section. Malone cannot be teased. The whole incident, however, is highly comic and threatens to end in broad, destructive farce. It is interesting to note that, whilst Sweeting remains the pleasantest of the three curates, Malone turns out to be more attractive than Donne.

Whatever underlying good nature there may have been in Charlotte Brontë's portrayal of the curates, there was none in her treatment of another of her ecclesiastics, Mr. Brocklehurst in *Jane Eyre*, based upon William Carus Wilson, the strict Calvinist founder of Cowan Bridge School. Mrs. Gaskell spoke, unadvisedly as it turned out, of Carus Wilson's character as it appeared to Charlotte Brontë when she wrote the latter's *Life*. There was an unseemly public controversy and she had to modify her remarks in the third edition. In her original statement, however, she referred to 'the wonderful fidelity with which [Charlotte Brontë represented] his disagreeable qualities, his spiritual pride, his love of power, his ignorance of human nature and consequent want of tenderness' (1st ed., I, 78). Something of these qualities can be detected in the account of Mr. Brocklehurst's first visit to Lowood School after the arrival of Jane Eyre.

II

'I find in settling accounts with the housekeeper, that a lunch, consisting of bread and cheese, has twice been served out to the girls during the past fortnight. How is this? I look over the regulations, and I find no such meal as lunch mentioned. Who introduced this innovation? and by what authority?'

'I must be responsible for the circumstance, sir,' replied Miss Temple: 'the breakfast was so ill-prepared that the pupils could not possibly eat it; and I dared not allow them to remain fasting till dinner-time.'

'Madam, allow me an instant. You are aware that my plan in bringing up these girls is, not to accustom them to habits of luxury and indulgence, but to render them hardy, patient, self-denying. Should any little accidental disappointment of the appetite occur, such as the spoiling of a meal, the under or the over-dressing of a dish, the incident ought not to be neutralised by replacing with something more delicate the comfort lost, thus pampering the body and obviating the aim of this institution; it ought to be improved to the spiritual edification of the pupils, by encouraging them to evince fortitude under the temporary privation. A brief address on those occasions would not be mistimed, wherein a judicious instructor would take the opportunity of referring to the sufferings of the primitive Christians; to the torments of martyrs; to the exhortations of Our Blessed Lord Himself, calling upon His disciples to take up their cross and follow Him; to His warnings that man shall not live by bread alone, but by every word that proceedeth out of the mouth of God; to His divine consolations, "If ye suffer hunger or thirst for My sake, happy are ye." Oh, madam, when you put bread and cheese, instead of burnt porridge, into these children's mouths, you may indeed feed their vile bodies, but you little think how you starve their immortal souls!' . . .

Meantime, Mr. Brocklehurst, standing on the hearth with his hands behind his back, majestically surveyed the whole school. Suddenly his eye gave a blink, as if it had met something that either dazzled or shocked its pupil; turning, he said in more rapid accents than he had hitherto used—

'Miss Temple, Miss Temple, what—*what* is that girl with curled hair? Red hair, ma'am, curled—curled all over?'

And extending his cane he pointed to the awful object, his hand shaking as he did so.

'It is Julia Severn,' replied Miss Temple very quietly.

'Julia Severn, ma'am! And why has she, or any other, curled hair? Why, in defiance of every precept and principle of this house, does she conform to the world so openly—here in an evangelical, charitable establishment—as to wear her hair one mass of curls?'

'Julia's hair curls naturally,' returned Miss Temple still more quietly.

'Naturally! Yes, but we are not conform to nature. I wish these girls to be the children of Grace: and why that abundance? I have again and again intimated that I desire the hair to be arranged closely, modestly, plainly. Miss Temple, the girl's hair must be cut off entirely; I will send a barber to-morrow: and I see others who have far too much of the excrescence—that tall girl, tell her to turn round. Tell all the first form to rise up and direct their faces to the wall.'

Miss Temple passed her handkerchief over her lips, as if to smooth away the involuntary smile that curled them. . . .

'All these top-knots must be cut off.'

Miss Temple seemed to remonstrate.

'Madam,' he pursued, 'I have a Master to serve whose kingdom is not of this world: my mission is to mortify in these girls the lusts of the flesh.' . . .

Mr. Brocklehurst was here interrupted; three other visitors, ladies, now entered the room. They ought to have come a little sooner to have heard his lecture on dress, for they were splendidly attired in velvet, silk, and furs. The two younger of the trio (fine girls of sixteen and seventeen) had gray beaver hats, then in fashion, shaded with ostrich plumes, and from under the brim of this graceful headdress fell a profusion of light tresses, elaborately curled; the elder lady was enveloped in a costly velvet shawl, trimmed with ermine, and she wore a false front of French curls.

Jane Eyre, ch. 7

Here Charlotte Brontë, by contrast with the passage from *Shirley*, depends extensively on direct speech as a means of self-revelation for her character. She also carefully but steadily heightens the impression of Brocklehurst's odious nature. He begins in an authoritative manner with his questions. He counters Miss Temple's reply with a repulsive condescension and then proceeds to a diatribe in which his crude opposition of body and soul becomes evident, the more so as in the latter part he turns to a partisan use of all the appropriate biblical texts and incidents, concluding with the offensive contrast of 'vile bodies' and 'immortal souls'.

Then the sanctimonious almost gives way to the comic. This is beautifully conveyed in the sudden alteration in Brocklehurst's behaviour, one moment 'majestically' surveying the school, the next blinking with shock; and in language so disjointed as to suggest that he is on the verge of apoplexy he points to Julia Severn's curls. Back again comes the Calvinistic jargon with its contrast of 'nature' and 'grace'; back again, but still more emphatically, emerges his insensitivity towards the girl. Charlotte Brontë again brings in the comic with Miss Temple's repression of a smile at Brocklehurst's order (and later the girl's grimace). This comedy is at once true to life, a reaction of that sanity that alone makes life bearable in such conditions, and a further reflection on Brocklehurst himself. It is the more effective as it precedes the most sanctimonious of all his outbursts, the climax by which Brocklehurst asserts his vicegerency for the Almighty ('I have a Master to serve whose kingdom is not of this world'). That climax, however, is but the prelude to superbly managed anti-climax, by which Brocklehurst is shown to be failing in this self-declared responsibilty at the point most close to him, namely, with his own family. His wife and daughters arrive, dressed not only in extravagant finery, but the daughters

43

with 'a profusion of light tresses, elaborately curled' and, oh most damning of all, their mother with 'a *false* front of French curls'.

After the two previous examples we may now turn to an example of straightforward description, that of Madame Beck, the proprietress of the school in *Villette*. The two paragraphs I choose come from the beginning and end of a passage, the remainder of which is concerned with a description of her school and the way she runs it.

12

When attired, Madame Beck appeared a personage of a figure rather short and stout, yet still graceful in its own peculiar way; that is, with the grace resulting from proportion of parts. Her complexion was fresh and sanguine, not too rubicund; her eye, blue and serene; her dark silk dress fitted her as a French sempstress alone can make a dress fit; she looked well, though a little bourgeoise; as bourgeoise, indeed, she was. I know not what of harmony pervaded her whole person; and yet her face offered contrast, too : its features were by no means such as are usually seen in conjunction with a complexion of such blended freshness and repose : their outline was stern : her forehead was high but narrow; it expressed capacity and some benevolence, but no expanse; nor did her peaceful yet watchful eye ever know the fire which is kindled in the heart or the softness which flows thence. Her mouth was hard : it could be a little grim; her lips were thin. For sensibility and genius, with all their tenderness and temerity, I felt somehow that Madame would be the right sort of Minos in petticoats. . . .

As Madame Beck ruled by espionage, she of course had her staff of spies : she perfectly knew the quality of the tools she used, . . . —I have known her fastidious in seeking pure metal for clean uses; and when once a bloodless and rustless instrument was found, she was careful of the prize, keeping it in silk and cotton-wool. Yet, woe be to that man or woman who relied on her one inch beyond the point where it was her interest to be trustworthy: interest was the master-key of Madame's nature—the main-spring of her motives—the alpha and omega of her life. I have seen her *feelings* appealed to, and I have smiled in half-pity, half-scorn at the appellants. . . . While devoid of sympathy, she had a sufficiency of rational benevolence: she would give in the readiest manner to people she had never seen—rather, however, to classes than to individuals. 'Pour les pauvres,' she opened her purse freely—against *the poor man*, as a rule, she kept it closed. . . . Not the agony in Gethsemane, not the death on Calvary, could have wrung from her eyes one tear.

Villette, ch. 8

This is a detailed description of physical appearance, and especially of the face. Physiognomic detail is seen to be important to Charlotte Brontë in other parts of her work. Notice the balance of the first paragraph, as it turns on the sentence which shows the narrator doubtful of har-mony, but certain of contrast, so that in the latter half of the paragraph we get a balance of qualities—the features are stern, the 'forehead high but narrow . . . some bene-volence but no expanse', etc. If anything, there is a harden-ing against Madame Beck as the analysis proceeds—her mouth 'hard', 'a little grim' and the lips 'thin', so that at the end we reach the ominous suggestion of a 'Minos in petticoats'.

Notice how the tentativeness of the first paragraph has been replaced by definite assertion in the last. There is a frightening power in the metaphor which gradually be-comes more precise—first a 'tool', then 'pure metal', and finally 'a bloodless and rustless instrument', with references to the sinister care by which it is preserved. Notice, too,

45

how the tentativeness that represented guesses from appearance is now the certainty that derives from interpretation of behaviour. Charlotte Brontë shows Madame Beck not as simply selfish but as more deeply motivated by interest, and then goes on to show how a sort of benevolence might in these circumstances be quite in character and yet terribly damning to the person who displays it. In this way *Villette* demonstrates something of its superiority over the other novels; psychological perception probes new depths.

Madame Beck also illustrates another recurrent feature of Charlotte Brontë's work—her fascination with the ominous and the evil. Even her heroes often have something rather frightening about them. Rochester is such a character, and in a different way so is M. Paul Emanuel in *Villette*. He does not have the conventional physical attractiveness of Rochester : indeed rather the opposite.

13

A dark little man he certainly was; pungent and austere. Even to me he seemed a harsh apparition, with his close-shorn, black head, his broad, sallow brow, his thin cheek, his wide and quivering nostril, his thorough glance and hurried bearing. Irritable he was; one heard that, as he apostrophised with vehemence the awkward squad under his orders.

Villette, ch. 14

M. Paul is probably the most subtly realised of all Charlotte Brontë's characters. He conducts his strange love-affair with Lucy through repeated insults and jealous friendship to a crisis at which his Roman Catholic friends seek to break the association. We need to trace this relationship in some detail to show that characterisation is not just a static, but can also be a developing phenomenon. In the earlier stages it is noticeable that Paul often insults Lucy when she is in the company of the attractive John Bretton.

46

His insults and jealousy spring from his egotism, and that in its turn is probably exaggerated by the awareness of his apparent lack of appeal by comparison with others. Paul's treatment of Lucy is developed throughout the most commonplace of situations.

In this passage Lucy speaks of Paul's teaching her arithmetic.

14

He did this at first with pleasure, indeed with unconcealed exultation, condescending to say that he believed I was 'bonne et pas trop faible' (*i.e.* well enough disposed, and not wholly destitute of parts) but, owing he supposed to adverse circumstances, 'as yet in a state of wretchedly imperfect mental development.'

The beginning of all effort has indeed with me been marked by a preternatural imbecility. I never could, even in forming a common acquaintance, assert or prove a claim to average quickness. A depressing and difficult passage has prefaced every new page I have turned in life.

So long as this passage lasted, M. Paul was very kind, very good, very forbearing; he saw the sharp pain inflicted, and felt the weighty humiliation imposed by my own sense of incapacity; and words can hardly do justice to his tenderness and helpfulness. His own eyes would moisten, when tears of shame and effort clouded mine; burdened as he was with work, he would steal half his brief space of recreation to give to me.

But, strange grief! when that heavy and overcast dawn began at last to yield to day; when my faculties began to struggle themselves free, and my time of energy and fulfilment came; when I voluntarily doubled, trebled, quadrupled the tasks he set, to please him as I thought, his kindness became sternness; the light changed in his eyes from a beam to a spark; he fretted, he opposed, he curbed me imperiously; the more I did, the harder I worked, the less he seemed content. . . .

Yet, when M. Paul sneered at me, I wanted to possess them more fully; his injustice stirred in me ambitious wishes—it imparted a strong stimulus—it gave wings to aspiration.

In the beginning, before I had penetrated to motives, that uncomprehended sneer of his made my heart ache, but by and by it only warmed the blood in my veins, and sent added action to my pulses. . . .

The combat was very sharp for a time. I seemed to have lost M. Paul's affection; he treated me strangely. In his most unjust moments he would insinuate that I had deceived him when I appeared, what he called 'faible'—that is incompetent; he said I had feigned a false incapacity. Again, he would turn suddenly round and accuse me of the most far-fetched imitations and impossible plagiarisms. . . .

Once, upon his preferring such an accusation, I turned upon him—I rose against him. Gathering an armful of his books out of my desk, filled my apron and poured them in a heap upon his estrade, at his feet. . . .

And returning to my desk, I laid my head on my arms, nor would I speak to him for two days afterwards. He pained and chagrined me. His affection had been very sweet and clear—a pleasure new and incomparable : now that this seemed withdrawn, I cared not for his lessons.

Villette, ch. 30

It is a mark of Charlotte Brontë's skill that she should have chosen something so mundane as this to give us so detailed a psychological encounter. There are two key words here—'affection' and 'combat'. The ideas they connote essentially involve at least two people, and the reader is struck by Lucy's awareness of herself and of her own response in this passage. Moreover, affection and combat are both progressive, and Charlotte Brontë suggests this progress very succinctly. In this case, too, the relationship is complex, and this also is brought out very well. We note Paul's tenderness ('His own eyes would moisten . . .'), and then the reaction towards harshness, paradoxically when there is evidence of some intellectual response on Lucy's part. This in its turn spurs Lucy on to a new determination. There then follows a passage which makes clear to the reader that he has been witnessing a dawning consciousness of the nature of the relationship; there is the reference to 'before I had penetrated to motives'. It is when Lucy has realised the position that the whole relationship, with its ebb and flow of affection and antagonism, is summarised in a paragraph that covers the phase of its most extreme expression. It is not surprising, therefore, that the sequel goes on to violence and counter-violence stated in the most direct and dramatic terms.

This is the prelude to their intimacy. Two short passages will illustrate their later developing relationship. The first is as follows:

15

He asked, by and by, if I would rather run to my companions than sit there? I said, no; I felt content to be where he was. He asked whether, if I were his sister, I should always be content to stay with a brother such as he. I said, I believed I should; and felt it. Again, he inquired whether, if he were to leave Villette, and go far away, I should be sorry; and I dropped Corneille, and made no reply.

'Petite sœur,' said he; 'how long could you remember me if we were separated?'

'That, Monsieur, I can never tell, because I do not know how long it will be before I shall cease to remember everything earthly.'

'If I were to go beyond seas for two—three—five years, should you welcome me on my return?'

'Monsieur, how could I live in the interval?'

'Pourtant j'ai été pour vous bien dur, bien exigeant.'

I hid my face with the book, for it was covered with tears. I asked him why he talked so; and he said he would talk so no more, and cheered me again with the kindest encouragement. Still, the gentleness with which he treated me during the rest of the day, went somehow to my heart. It was too tender. It was mournful. I would rather he had been abrupt, whimsical, and irate as was his wont.

Villette, ch. 33

And the second:

16

'Now, Mademoiselle Lucy, look at me, and with that truth which I believe you never knowingly violate, answer me one question. Raise your eyes; rest them on mine; have no hesitation; fear not to trust me—I am a man to be trusted.'

I raised my eyes.

'Knowing me thoroughly now—all my antecedents, all my responsibilities—having long known my faults, can you and I still be friends?'

'If monsieur wants a friend in me, I shall be glad to have a friend in him.'

'But a close friend I mean—intimate and real—kindred in all but blood? Will Miss Lucy be the sister of a very poor, fettered, burdened, encumbered man?'

I could not answer him in words, yet I suppose I *did* answer him; he took my hand, which found comfort in the shelter of his. *His* friendship was not a doubtful, wavering benefit—a cold, distant hope—a sentiment so brittle as not to bear the weight of a finger: I at once felt (or *thought* I felt) its support like that of some rock.

Villette, ch. 35

In these passages Charlotte Brontë seeks to convey Paul's sincerity and his restraint. Notice the references to only a brotherly relationship, his recognition of his previous severity, and the countering recognition by Lucy of his present overwhelming, even pathetically overwhelming, tenderness. Notice also how in the second passage the intimacy has become still closer. If anything, the tone is quieter here, but somehow more certain. A comparison of the two final paragraphs will reveal the greater simplicity, the greater deliberateness of structure in the latter, and the final image, commonplace as it is, comes with absolute appropriateness.

Paul's Roman Catholic friends sought to break the association, but in vain. At the end he installs Lucy as head of a school and he himself goes off for three years: 'Lucy take my love. One day share my life. Be my dearest, first on earth' (chapter 41). It is a strange end to a strange tale, the most complex of all Charlotte Brontë's studies of human relationships, in which personal idiosyncrasy and the difficulties of religious differences are overcome by depth of affection. The end is strange because the words I have quoted do not end the story. In fact, without saying so explicitly, Charlotte Brontë leaves a broad enough hint that M. Paul died at sea on his way home after years away from Lucy. Mrs. Gaskell informs us that Charlotte's father wanted a happy ending, but 'she could no more alter her fictitious ending than if they had been facts that she was relating. All she could do in compliance with her father's wish was so to veil his fate in oracular words as to leave it to the character and discernment of her readers to interpret her meaning' (*Life of Charlotte Brontë*, 1st ed., II, 266).

Charlotte Brontë's other major male character is Rochester in *Jane Eyre*. His is a history of sin and redemption. Before his entry he is said to be 'rather peculiar' and at Jane's first meeting with him she notices his 'dark face, with stern features and a heavy brow'. He turns out to be 'a man with a past', and his immoral life in Paris would no doubt add both mystery and repulsion to him for many Victorian readers. But then Charlotte Brontë very cunningly placed the revelation of his history at a point where Jane had already become interested in him and he in her; and in addition, there are compensating factors for his behaviour and the nobility of his accepting responsibility for his mistress's child, Adèle, who is almost certainly not his. The compensating factor of greatest importance is the marriage into which he has been trapped, but we only learn of that later. There is a certain melodrama in the whole Céline Varens episode with its history of infatuation, unfaithfulness, and a duel, but yet it is of a piece with the general exaggeration of Rochester's character. It is interesting to see, too, how there is a continuing suggestion that Rochester is never really debased. Thus when he recognises the rival who is receiving Céline's favours, he says:

'The fang of the snake jealousy was instantly broken; because at the same time my love for Céline sank under an extinguisher. A woman who could betray me for such a rival was not worth contending for; she deserved only scorn—less, however, than I, who had been her dupe.'

Jane Eyre, ch. 15

Despite the modesty of the last words, we must nevertheless feel that we have only Rochester's word for it, and that word is at times artificially heightened as the first phrase of this extract shows. It is Jane's sympathy towards Rochester that saves him for us.

Rochester's mistresses are important, for they are what he might have made Jane. He so far felt her nobility as to prefer bigamy to a liaison of this kind, but after the attempt at marriage has been stopped and he has told her of the way in which he had been entrapped into his original marriage the question of his past mistresses recurs. Now, however, Rochester is talking of the way in which he hated the recollection of the time he spent with mistresses. Nonetheless the dialogue reaches the climax of a like suggestion, to be differentiated only in that this time there will be love in the relationship. One can appreciate Rochester's soul-searing problem. Even at the earlier stage, as he contemplates bigamy, he argues his claims to a better fate.

'Is the wandering and sinful, but now rest-seeking and repentant, man justified in daring the world's opinion, in order to attach to him for ever this gentle, gracious, genial stranger, thereby securing his own peace of mind and regeneration of life?'

Jane Eyre, ch. 20

After the prevention of the 'marriage' his appeal reaches its height in the following passage.

17

'Jane you understand what I want of you? Just this promise —"I will be yours, Mr. Rochester."'

'Mr. Rochester, I will *not* be yours.'

Another long silence.

'Jane!' recommenced he, with a gentleness that broke me down with grief, and turned me stone-cold with ominous terror—for this still voice was the pant of a lion rising— 'Jane, do you mean to go one way in the world, and to let me go another?'

'I do.'

'Jane' (bending towards and embracing me), 'do you mean it now?'

'I do.'

'And now?' softly kissing my forehead and cheek.

'I do,' extricating myself from restraint rapidly and completely.

'Oh, Jane, this is bitter! This—this is wicked. It would not be wicked to love me.'

'It would to obey you.' . . .

'What shall I do, Jane? Where turn for a companion, and for some hope?'

'Do as I do: trust in God and yourself. Believe in heaven. Hope to meet again there.'

'Then you will not yield?'

'No.'

'Then you condemn me to live wretched, and to die accursed?' His voice rose.

'I advise you to live sinless, and I wish you to die tranquil.'

Jane Eyre, ch. 27

This of course, is action, but, as I have said, we cannot divorce character from action, least of all in the most successful passages. This extract, in fact, dramatises the abstraction of the preceding one. In the repeated short and simple appeals we have the demonstration of Rochester's misery and his passion, and, if anything, much as the Victorians may have been impressed by Jane's moral integrity, he emerges from the encounter more human than she. Her last speech, in particular, balanced so precisely as almost to appear epigrammatic, is cold beside his passionate appeals.

They part, not to be reunited until he has suffered terribly. In trying to rescue his mad wife, the person at the root of all his troubles, from the fire she had started Rochester suffers the loss of hand and eyes. His maiming is the price he has had to pay for his sins, his sacrifice is the mark of his redemption. His reward is reunion with Jane (see above, pp. 18–21). The final chapter of *Jane Eyre* refers to the later histories of all the major characters.

Rochester is rewarded by a partial recovery. One wonders whether it might have left a more authentic, if sadder, note if he had remained blind. The end of *Villette* is much more doubtful. Here in *Jane Eyre*, however, the sufferer recovers, and his reward is to see his son, significantly a boy and 'his first-born', recalling the age-long desire to perpetuate one's name, and a boy like his father, fulfilling the concomitant desire for offspring after one's own likeness. Being so blessed, it is of a piece with Charlotte Brontë's (and Jane Eyre's) view of things that Rochester thanks God, that is, that he reacts in a religious direction.

In both *Jane Eyre* and *Villette* there is another man, in a number of obvious ways more eligible than the hero as a suitor—St. John Rivers and John Graham Bretton respectively. Bretton is not attracted by Lucy, and this is in character, for he seems altogether too conventional and too superficial. His main importance is to provide opportunities for outbursts of M. Paul's jealousy, whilst she is able to keep him in touch with, and explain various aspects of the behaviour of, the flirtatious Ginevra Fanshawe, to whom he is attracted. He has none of Paul's passion, and it is perhaps only in this negative way that he is important to the main characters.

St. John Rivers is not without passion, but his is a cold passion, expressed in his ruthless dedication of himself to a missionary life. If Brocklehurst seems to represent one, and that a repulsive, form of Victorian Evangelicalism, Rivers may be said to represent another, that form of Evangelical heroism which took the Christian gospel to the four corners of the earth at a tremendous cost in personal sacrifice. In pursuit of his ideal St. John destroys all feeling for himself and is led to expect from others a similar self-abnegation. Others, in fact, have to become slaves of his intent. It is in this frame of mind that he proposes marriage to Jane. Whereas Rochester wanted Jane in love without marriage, St. John suggests marriage without love.

18

'And what does *your* heart say?' demanded St. John.

'My heart is mute—my heart is mute,' I answered, struck and thrilled.

'Then I must speak for it,' continued the deep, relentless

voice. 'Jane, come with me to India: come as my helpmeet and fellow-labourer.'

The glen and sky spun round: the hills heaved! It was as if I had heard a summons from Heaven—as if a visionary messenger, like him of Macedonia, had enounced, 'Come over and help us!' . . .

'Oh, St. John!' I cried, 'have some mercy!'

I appealed to one who, in the discharge of what he believed his duty, knew neither mercy nor remorse. He continued—

'God and nature intended you for a missionary's wife. It is not personal, but mental endowments they have given you: you are formed for labour, not for love. A missionary's wife you must—shall be. You shall be mine: I claim you—not for my pleasure, but for my Sovereign's service.'

'I am not fit for it: I have no vocation,' I said. . . .

As he leaned back against the crag behind him, folded his arms on his chest, and fixed his countenance, I saw he was prepared for a long and trying opposition, . . . — resolved, however, that that close should be conquest for him.

'Humility, Jane,' said he, 'is the groundwork of Christian virtues: you say right that you are not fit for the work. Who is fit for it? . . . I, for instance, am but dust and ashes. With St. Paul, I acknowledge myself the chiefest of sinners; but I do not suffer this sense of my personal vileness to daunt me. I know my Leader: . . . Think like me, Jane —trust like me. It is the Rock of Ages I ask you to lean on: do not doubt but it will bear the weight of your human weakness.'

Jane Eyre, ch. 34

The passage begins with that intense direction towards the self, that Evangelical mode which is never far from an invitation to self-accusation. Its counterpart is the certainty which proceeds from the interlocutor ('Then I must speak for it'), that confidence of speaking on behalf of the Almighty ('God and nature intended . . .'), that assertion that the person addressed will be giving themselves up to God ('for my Sovereign's service'). Even the use of the image in this last phrase is typical. In the final speech we notice also the Evangelical's favourite device of self-abnegation and then of automatic avowal of God's power. By the time we reach the end the speech has given way to cliché and moralising. There is even something characteristic in the way in which St. John's physical attitude is described in the penultimate paragraph. And the setting of glen and sky, of hills and crags contributes its own appropriate ruggedness to the scene. Jane's cry for mercy would not penetrate so unassailable a heart. St. John 'knew neither mercy nor remorse'. Typically, he pursued his dedicated martyr's path. The book ends with three paragraphs devoted to St. John, the tone of which is evidence enough of the admiration Charlotte Brontë had for such noble, if uncomfortable, souls. On this a comment will be made in a later section (see below, pp. 108–9).

As there is a contrast of male characters, so also there is usually a foil for the heroines. The foil is usually beautiful in appearance, if superficial in character. Blanche Ingram in *Jane Eyre* and Ginevra Fanshawe in *Villette* are two of a kind. Both seem to prosper whilst the heroine either suffers or at best makes no progress. Ginevra plays a continuous part in *Villette*. She has, as it were, a separate and contrasting history to that of the heroine. Because she is so shallow, Charlotte Brontë does not make much of an attempt to analyse her character; the effort would not be worthwhile. Instead, she shows her through action, through encounter with first one man, then another. In particular, she shows the effect that she has on John Bretton. In one passage in which she is discussing him with Lucy under his pseudonym of Isidore (an identification not to be discovered by the reader until later in the book) we read :

'Perhaps, however, you now feel certain that you will be able to marry M. Isidore; your parents and uncle have given their consent, and, for your part, you love him entirely?'

'Mais pas du tout!' (she always had recourse to French when about to say something specially heartless and perverse). 'Je suis sa reine, mais il n'est pas mon roi.'

'Excuse me, I must believe this language is mere nonsense and coquetry.' . . .

'Try to get a clear idea of the state of your mind. To me it seems in a great mess—chaotic as a rag-bag.'

'It is something in this fashion,' she cried out ere long: 'the man is too romantic and devoted, and he expects something more of me than I find it convenient to be. He thinks I am perfect: furnished with all sorts of sterling qualities and solid virtues, such as I never had, nor intended to have. Now, one can't help in his presence, rather trying to justify his good opinion; and it does so tire one to be goody, and to talk sense—for he really thinks I am sensible. I am far more at my ease with you, old lady—you, you dear crosspatch—who take me at my lowest, and know me to be coquettish, and ignorant, and flirting, and fickle, and silly, and selfish, and all the other sweet things you and I have agreed to be a part of my character.'

Villette, ch. 9

The opposition provided by Lucy's seriousness brings out Ginevra's levity extremely well. Notice the insistence in the words 'try to get a clear idea of the state of your mind'. Notice too how convincingly 'heartless and perverse' Ginevra seems when she changes to French and so concisely sums up the relatioship in the sentence 'Je suis sa reine, mais il n'est pas mon roi'. 'Mere nonsense and coquetry' Lucy pretends that it is, but the juxtaposition tells the reader that it is far otherwise. When Ginevra does assess the whole matter in the final paragraph, we see, in fact, a degree of self-knowledge that might seem surprising. It is this and the consequent low estimate of herself that makes Ginevra appear by no means so heartless as at times she might be thought. Nevertheless, hers is the world of passing pleasure, and in one short paragraph Charlotte Brontë summarises this admirably.

20

Ginevra Fanshawe was the belle, the fairest and the gayest present; she was selected to open the ball: very lovely she looked, very gracefully she danced, very joyously she smiled. Such scenes were her triumphs—she was the child of pleasure. Work or suffering found her listless and dejected, powerless and repining; but gaiety expanded her butterfly's wings, lit up their gold-dust and bright spots, made her flash like a gem, and flush like a flower. At all ordinary diet and plain beverage she would pout; but she fed on creams and ices like a humming-bird on honey-paste; sweet wine was her element, and sweet cake her daily bread. Ginevra lived her full life in a ballroom; elsewhere she drooped dispirited.

Villette, ch. 14

In this passage one notices the reliance upon the accumulation of adjectives and adverbs in the first part, and then of imagery in the second. Note the contrast of the words—pleasure has 'belle, fairest, gayest, lovely, gracefully, joyously', work has 'listless and dejected, powerless and pining'. The imagery begins with the emphasis on the beautiful and gay, but the choice of the butterfly hints that it is also the ephemeral. There is a range of imagery, with varying degrees of power. The butterfly image is not only first, it is most prominent, but it is supported by references to a gem and a flower. The subsidiary role of these two images is evident from their generic rather than specific denotations. There follows the developed image of eating,

59

again with contrast, but the contrast is merely to act as a prelude, first a reference to 'ordinary diet and plain beverage' in order that what follows may build up the impression of luxury. Finally, in a neatly divided sentence Charlotte Brontë completes the description of Ginevra's own deeply divided response to the demands of life.

Blanche Ingram in *Jane Eyre* is also beautiful, but hers is a different, and in many ways, less important role. Her beauty contrasts with Jane's lesser endowments in this regard, and she is used in a temporary phase as a rival, and more likely successful rival, for Rochester's hand, whilst Jane nurses what she conceives to be a hopeless passion in silence. Mrs. Fairfax describes Blanche Ingram's beauty more fully than we ever find Ginevra's.

21

'Tall, fine bust, sloping shoulders; long, graceful neck; olive complexion, dark and clear; noble features; eyes rather like Mr. Rochester's, large and black, and as brilliant as her jewels. And then she had such a fine head of hair, raven-black, and so becomingly arranged; a crown of thick plaits behind, and in front the longest, the glossiest curls I ever saw. She was dressed in pure white; an amber-coloured scarf was passed over her shoulder and across her breast, tied at the side, and descending in long, fringed ends below her knee. She wore an amber-coloured flower, too, in her hair: it contrasted well with the jetty mass of her curls.'

Jane Eyre, ch. 16

The description serves to make Jane re-consider what she takes to be her illusions and to suggest to herself that she draw two portraits to look at in order to check the recurrence of such illusions in future, one of herself, 'Portrait of a Governess, disconnected, poor, and plain', the other in the terms of Mrs. Fairfax's description:

'Recall the august yet harmonious lineaments, the Grecian

neck and bust; let the round and dazzling arm be visible, and the delicate hand; omit neither diamond ring nor gold bracelet; portray carefully the attire, aerial lace and glistening satin, graceful scarf and golden rose; call it "Blanche, an accomplished Lady of rank".'

ibid.

Between this and Mrs. Fairfax's account the description of Blanche Ingram has gone through the crucible of Jane's emotions. The structure of the sentences, selection and force of the adjectives and the effect of additional detail in this latter passage make all the difference. Jane disavows jealousy, claiming in a later passage that between herself and Blanche Ingram there was no comparison in things that matter : 'her mind was poor, her heart barren'.

Heroines

With the exception of *The Professor*, Charlotte Brontë's works are centred upon what happens to a woman, or, in the case of *Shirley*, two women. There may therefore be a special value in devoting a separate section of this study to her heroines.

Charlotte Brontë isolates these figures often by means of the journey and separation. This is most pronounced in *Jane Eyre* where her pilgrimage takes Jane from Gateshead to Lowood to Thornfield to Moor House and finally to Ferndean, but in *Villette* (and for that matter with Crimsworth in *The Professor*) the main character moves from England to the peculiarly isolating environment of a foreign land. Even Shirley may be said to be lonely in a crowd. It is only her self-sufficiency that strengthens and sustains her in what is rarely a hospitable and sometimes a hostile environment. In an absolute sense, life is a journey also for these characters in their search for contact and quest for happiness.

Jane Eyre begins with the heroine's description of herself as an outcast child, excluded from the family circle of the aunt and the cousins with whom she lives.

22

> The said Eliza, John, and Georgina were now clustered
> round their mamma in the drawing-room : she lay reclined
> on a sofa by the fireside, and with her darlings about her
> (for the time neither quarrelling nor crying) looked per-
> fectly happy. Me, she had dispensed from joining the group,
> saying, 'She regretted to be under the necessity of keeping
> me at a distance; but that until she heard from Bessie, and
> could discover by her own observation that I was endeav-
> ouring in good earnest to acquire a more sociable and child-
> like disposition, a more attractive and sprightly manner—
> something lighter, franker, more natural, as it were—she
> really must exclude me from privileges intended only for
> contented, happy little children.'

Jane Eyre, ch. 1

No reasons are given for this exclusion, only assertions.
The orphan child, the one most in need of protection, is
cast aside, whilst the other children are favoured. The self-
righteous tone of Mrs. Reed is transferred to the report in
the last sentence; one notices the force of 'really' and the
echo of the adult voice in the phrase 'contented, happy
little children'.

This is but the prelude to all Jane's sufferings as a child.
They begin with her unjust punishment for her retaliation
against John Reed's attack upon her. She is banished to the
red-room (see below pp. 89–90) there to contemplate what
had occurred.

23

> My head still ached and bled with the blow and fall I had
> received; no one had reproved John for wantonly striking
> me; and because I had turned against him to avert further
> irrational violence, I was loaded with general oppro-
> brium.
>   'Unjust!—unjust!' said my reason, forced by the agonis-

ing stimulus into precocious though transitory power; and Resolve, equally wrought up, instigated some strange expedient to achieve escape from insupportable oppression—as running away, or, if that could not be effected, never eating or drinking more, and letting myself die.

What a consternation of soul was mine that dreary afternoon! How all my brain was in tumult, and all my heart in insurrection! Yet in what darkness, what dense ignorance, was the mental battle fought! I could not answer the ceaseless inward question—*why* I thus suffered; now, at the distance of—I will not say how many years—I see it clearly.

I was a discord in Gateshead Hall; I was like nobody there; I had nothing in harmony with Mrs. Reed or her children, or her chosen vassalage. If they did not love me, in fact, as little did I love them. They were not bound to regard with affection a thing that could not sympathise with one amongst them; a heterogenous thing, opposed to them in temperament, in capacity, in propensities; a useless thing, incapable of serving their interest, or adding to their pleasure; a noxious thing, cherishing the germs of indignation at their treatment, of contempt of their judgement.

Jane Eyre, ch. 2

Here is all the child's sense of outrage and injustice. The child-mind is evoked in such resolutions as 'never eating or drinking more', and yet this account is obviously told across the gap of years, which helps to put it in perspective. The strongly abstract quality of the first part of the second paragraph—'reason' and 'Resolve' as subjects and phrases such as 'agonising stimulus', 'precocious though transitory power', 'instigated some strange expedient'—almost goes too far in insisting that the narrator is an adult. The whole passage follows a familiar Brontëan pattern—first the event, then the immediate reaction to it, followed by a description of the feeling that developed from that reaction, and finally an assessment of the overall situation which explains why the event happened in the first place. The last paragraph is therefore more reflective than the rest. And yet it also has a rhetorical note, exemplified in the repeated 'thing', each time with a different adjectival and phrasal context, the whole being made to emphasise the oppression and hatred of the Reeds against Jane.

This sense of oppression which Jane first feels at Gateshead continues through her schooldays. Indeed, the transition from Gateshead to Lowood is marked by a vicious report upon her before the whole school by Mr. Brocklehurst. Although she claims that the later years at Lowood were pleasant enough, these are rather sketchily treated, and it is not until she reaches Thornfield that what to the reader is a convincingly pleasanter phase of her life begins. Even here, however, she is isolated. Her very position as governess, superior to the servants but inferior (and Blanche Ingram makes sure that Jane knows this) to the household, emphasises this. This isolation is further stressed by Jane's apparently hopeless love (cf. the remarks on Blanche Ingram above, pp. 60–1). In this section of the novel Charlotte Brontë provides an excellent statement of the fluctuations of Jane's feelings.

24

Did I say, a few days since, that I had nothing to do with him but to receive my salary at his hands? Did I forbid myself to think of him in any other light than as a paymaster? Blasphemy against nature! Every good, true, vigorous feeling I have gathers impulsively round him. I know I must conceal my sentiments: I must smother hope; I must remember that he cannot care much for me. For when I say that I am of his kind, I do not mean that I have his force to influence, and his spell to attract; I mean only that I have certain tastes and feelings in common with him I must, then, repeat continually that we are for ever sun dered—and yet, while I breathe and think, I must love him.'

Jane Eyre, ch. 17

In this passage of interior monologue there is a vigorous intensity created by exclamation, rhetorical questions, short sentences and, above all, repeated references in the first person. There is also the power of balanced sentences ('I must conceal my sentiments; I must smother hope; I must remember . . .'), of contrasting parts ('I do not mean . . . , I mean only . . .'), of accumulation ('Every good, true, vigorous feeling . . .'), of the insistent verb of necessity ('must'). This personal intensity contrasts markedly with the conventional and superficial social attitudes of the other characters described in the same passage.

Even more passionate is Jane's declaration to Rochester when she thinks that he is about to marry Blanche Ingram.

25

'Do you think I can stay to become nothing to you? Do you think I am an automaton?—a machine without feelings? and can bear to have my morsel of bread snatched from my lips, and my drop of living water dashed from my cup? Do you think, because I am poor, obscure, plain, and little, I am soulless and heartless? You think wrong!— I have as much soul as you—and full as much heart! And if God had gifted me with some beauty and much wealth, I should have made it as hard for you to leave me as it is now for me to leave you. I am not talking to you now through the medium of custom, conventionalities, nor even of mortal flesh;—it is my spirit that addresses your spirit; just as if both had passed through the grave, and we stood at God's feet, equal,—as we are!'

Jane Eyre, ch. 23

This is a critical moment, for, hopeless though Jane feels her love to have been throughout, she has had the benefit of Rochester's presence. Now that he is apparently giving himself to another she feels that she cannot stay. Her short-lived and perhaps illusory attempt at contact is to be broken and her wanderings must begin again. High passion can easily overreach itself and, especially in the novel, become ridiculous. Here indeed it may be overstretched in its language a little at times ('the morsel of bread' and 'drop of living water' are much like excessive self-dramatising), and there is a hint of the stilted in the latter part of the passage. Nevertheless, we can believe that this is spirit speaking to spirit. (For quotation at length of this episode, see below pp. 99–100.)

There follows the proposal, the 'wedding' and the disaster. Jane flees from Rochester. The following passage describes her thoughts as she wanders.

26

I skirted fields and hedges and lanes till after sunrise. I believe it was a lovely summer morning: I know my shoes, which I had put on when I left the house, were soon wet with dew. But I looked neither to rising sun, nor smiling sky, nor wakening nature. He who is taken out to pass through a fair scene to the scaffold, thinks not of the flowers that smile on his road, but of the block and axe-edge; of the disseverment of bone and vein; of the grave gaping at the end: and I thought of drear flight and homeless wandering—and oh! with agony I thought of what I left. I could not help it. I thought of him now—in his room—watching the sunrise; hoping I should soon come to say I would stay with him and be his. I longed to be his; I panted to return: it was not too late. I could yet spare him the bitter pang of bereavement. As yet my flight, I was sure, was undiscovered. I could go back and be his comforter—his pride; his redeemer from misery, perhaps from ruin. Oh, that fear of his self-abandonment—far worse than my abandonment—how it goaded me! It was a barbed arrowhead in my breast; it tore me when I

67

tried to extract it; it sickened me when remembrance thrust it farther in. Birds began singing in brake and copse : birds were faithful to their mates; birds were emblems of love. What was I? In the midst of my pain of heart and frantic effort of principle, I abhorred myself. I had no solace from self-approbation : none even from self-respect. I had injured —wounded—left my master. I was hateful in my own eyes. Still I could not turn, nor retrace one step. God must have led me on. As to my own will or conscience, impassioned grief had trampled one and stifled the other. I was weeping wildly as I walked along my solitary way; fast, fast I went like one delirious. A weakness, beginning inwardly, extending to the limbs, seized me, and I fell; I lay on the ground some minutes, pressing my face to the wet turf. I had some fear—or hope—that here I should die; but I was soon up, crawling forwards on my hands and knees, and then again raised to my feet—as eager and as determined as ever to reach the road.

Jane Eyre, ch. 27

Again, Charlotte Brontë shows her skill in building up the emotional impression of a scene, the more so because here we have to rely on what Jane Eyre says about herself and, moreover, *reports* about herself. Even the immediacy of narrative in the present is missing. She begins with her feeling of partial oblivion, unaware of the beauties of the summer morning ('I believe . . . But I looked neither to . . .'), an oblivion ascribed to her misery, which is expressed indirectly, but powerfully, in the detailed image of the condemned criminal on the way to execution. She then quite suddenly, and even one feels irrationally, returns strongly to herself ('I thought of drear flight and homeless wandering'), but this is momentary. She reverts to thought of Rochester whom she cannot forget. She merely says that she thought of herself, but of him it is 'and oh! with agony I thought'. Agony is one stage in the rising emotion. It is followed by desire ('I longed to be his; I panted to return').

This brings in the conflict ('I could go back'), and by going back she might save him from ruin. His likely sufferings return upon her with redoubled force. The statement has now brought us to a realisation of the complex and soul-rending position that Jane is in. This is then symbolised by the extremely effective image of 'the barbed arrow-head', creating pain whatever is done with it. And at this moment of intense agony she becomes aware of the birds, symbols of the natural order, of harmony, happiness, faithfulness and love, commenting in all-unknowing irony on the human disorder. She is sent back to herself, directly and pointedly to herself ('What was I?'), to give the answer 'I abhorred myself' and to repeat it, 'I was hateful in my own eyes'. This is the intensity to which the episode has risen, when at this point a new consideration enters—'God must have led me on'. She is at the point of delirium and physical collapse. No more is said about God's leading. It is uncomfortable to think about when powerful human considerations point in another direction, but it is inescapable. Events have to move that way. This is the tragic quality—destiny irresistible.

At the end Jane is supernaturally driven to return to Rochester. After they are re-united (see above, pp. 18–21), he describes his call to her at the very time that she had thought she heard that call. The supernatural, though sparingly used, is of a piece with the novel. It is the outward manifestation of divine disposition. Jane had to leave Rochester by destiny irresistible, but Charlotte Brontë believed that 'in the midst of judgment, [God] has remembered mercy'. We need to remember the essentially religious quality of her outlook. The reunion of Jane and Rochester is marked by his adoption of a similar outlook. This comes rather suddenly, but we need as well to remember that it is all placed within the supernatural context. Jane and her beloved are one at last.

Victorian heroines, like the children of that time, seem in general to have been more often seen than heard. They were not to be in the least assertive, but for passivity Lucy Snowe must surely be among the best examples. Her modesty is extreme.

In the following passage she tells of her shyness and lack of self-confidence when M. Paul suggests that along with some of the girl-students she should improvise a composition in French in public.

27

I knew what the result of such an experiment would be. I, to whom nature had denied the impromptu faculty; who, in public, was by nature a cypher; whose time of mental activity, even when alone, was not under the meridian sun; who needed the fresh silence of morning, or the recluse peace of evening, to win from the Creative Impulse one evidence of his presence, one proof of his force; I, with whom that Impulse was the most intractable, the most capricious, the most maddening of masters (him before me always excepted)—a deity which sometimes, under circumstances apparently propitious, would not speak when questioned, would not hear when appealed to, would not, when sought, be found; but would stand, all cold, all indurated, all granite, a dark Baal with carven lips and blank eyeballs, and breast like the stone face of a tomb; and again, suddenly at some turn, some sound, some long-trembling sob of the wind, at some rushing past of an unseen stream of electricity, the irrational demon would wake unsolicited, would stir strangely alive, would rush from its pedestal like a perturbed Dagon, calling to its votary for a sacrifice, whatever the hour—to its victim for some blood or some breath, whatever the circumstance or scene—rousing its priest, treacherously promising vaticination, perhaps filling its temple with a strange hum of oracles, but sure to give half the significance to fateful winds, and grudging to the desperate listener even a miserable remnant—yielding it sordidly, as though each world had been a drop of the deathless ichor of its own dark veins.

Villette, ch. 30

There is a certain paradox here in that this extract represents a positive onrush of eloquence in a single unstoppable sentence. It displays both a variety and intensity of reference. First, there is that gentle, pleasant reference of 'the fresh silence of morning, or the recluse peace of evening', but this is soon followed by reference to powerful, compulsive forces. The epithets are strong, gathered in groups and intensified ('intractable', 'capricious', 'maddening' and each with a 'most' before it; 'cold', 'indurated', 'granite', each with 'all' before it). The Impulse is compared to fierce and bloody pagan deities ('a dark Baal', 'a perturbed Dagon. calling to its votary for a sacrifice'). There is a suggestion of delusion by this compelling force, and finally a hint of slow and painful possession, with Lucy as the unwilling medium expressing the words of the Creative Impulse, a devil of 'dark veins', a devil eternal filled with 'deathless ichor'.

Lucy, like Jane Eyre, is a lonely character, but it is in her passivity that she differs from Jane. This seems to give an additional dimension to her introspection as compared with Jane. The latter often meditates on what she has done or not done or should do in relation to her circumstances. Lucy seems more aware of what she is and continues to be at a fundamental level of character. This comes out pointedly in the following passage.

28

Oh, my childhood! I had feelings: passive as I lived, little as I spoke, cold as I looked, when I thought of past days, I *could* feel. About the present, it was better to be stoical; about the future—such a future as mine—to be dead. And in catalepsy and a dead trance, I studiously held the quick of my nature. . . .

I did long, achingly, then and for four-and-twenty hours afterwards, for something to fetch me out of my present existence, and lead me upwards and onwards. This longing, and all of a similar kind, it was necessary to knock on the head; which I did, figuratively, after the manner of Jael to Sisera, driving a nail through their temples. Unlike Sisera, they did not die: they were but transiently stunned, and at intervals would turn on the nail with a rebellious wrench: then did the temples bleed, and the brain thrill to its core.

To-night, I was not so mutinous, nor so miserable. My Sisera lay quiet in the tent, slumbering; and if his pain ached through his slumbers, something like an angel—the ideal —knelt near, dropping balm on the soothed temples, holding before the sealed eyes a magic glass, of which the sweet, solemn visions were repeated in dreams, and shedding a reflex from her moonlight wings and robe over all the transfixed sleeper, over the tent threshold, over the landscape lying without. Jael, the stern woman, sat apart, relenting somewhat over her captive; but more prone to dwell on the faithful expectation of Heber coming home. By which words I mean that the cool peace and dewy sweetness of the night filled me with a mood of hope: not hope on any definite point, but a general sense of encouragement and heart-ease.

Villette, ch. 12

Notice the stress on such words as 'passive', 'cold', 'stoical', 'dead' and how in the first paragraph past, present and future are embraced in this survey of passivity. It gives all the greater poignancy to the longing, which has likewise to be suppressed. Here the Biblical image, recalling one of the cruellest incidents imaginable, (see Judges V, 17–21), is particularly powerful and suggestive of the punishment which Lucy has to inflict upon herself. In fact, Charlotte Brontë heightens the excruciating experience with reference that is not found in the Biblical story such as turning 'on the nail with a rebellious wrench: [and] then did the temples bleed, and the brain thrill to its core'. After the description of such suffering, the relief of the present incident is all the more pleasant. This is one of the most extended parallels in Charlotte Brontë's work, and serves not only to provide an effective image of psychological stress but to set it in such primitive terms as to remind us how close we all are always to the point of breakdown.

It is therefore exactly right that a central episode in Lucy's history should be a nervous breakdown. I have already referred to the point at which it actually strikes her (see p. 26 above). Its onset is preceded by a horrible dream.

29

By the clock of St. Jean Baptiste, that dream remained scarce fifteen minutes—a brief space, but sufficing to wring my whole frame with unknown anguish; to confer a nameless experience that had the hue, the mien, the terror, the very tone of a visitation from eternity. Between twelve and one that night a cup was forced to my lips, black, strong, strange, drawn from no well, but filled up seething from a bottomless and boundless sea. Suffering, brewed in temporal or calculable measure, and mixed for mortal lips, tastes not as this suffering tasted. Having drank and woke, I thought all was over: the end came and passed by. . . . Some fearful hours went over me: indescribably was I torn, racked, and oppressed in mind. Amidst the horrors of that dream I think the worst lay here. Methought the well-loved dead, who had loved *me* well in life, met me elsewhere, alienated: galled was my inmost spirit with an unutterable sense of despair about the future. Motive there was none why I should try to recover or wish to live; and yet quite unendurable was the pitiless and haughty voice in which Death challenged me to engage his unknown terrors. When I tried to pray I could only utter these words:

'From my youth up Thy terrors have I suffered with a troubled mind.'

Most true was it.

Villette, ch. 15

This is a translation of thought as it is expressed in the previous passages into the dramatisation of dream. The reflective is transformed into the horrific. Notice the stress on the incomprehensible—'unknown anguish', 'a nameless experience'. Notice too the grotesque, concentrating upon the two terrifying details—the cup, with its suggestion of witches, but then, transcending these, by drawing our attention to the seething of the bottomless and boundless sea. All this has the conviction of deranged experience. It is followed by conscious suffering, by recognition of isolation and the description of 'fearful hours . . . torn, racked and oppressed in mind'. With what accuracy, too, Charlotte Brontë reproduces exactly the most terrible experience for one so lonely as Lucy. The only affection she could draw upon was that of recollection, of those who had loved her and were now dead. And even they, in the dream, repudiated her! This was the moment of total despair. Disowned by the past, totally isolated in the present, how could there be any future?

Again Lucy has recourse to Scripture, or, rather, to the Prayer Book version of Psalm XXXVIII, verse 15. This is a nightmare psalm, and it is more than the quotation of this verse that Charlotte Brontë must have had in mind. It needs no more than quotation to feel the appositeness of sentences such as 'my life draweth nigh unto hell' (v. 3), 'Thou hast laid me in the lowest pit: in a place of darkness, and in the deep' (v. 5), and thinking first of the sea reference, 'They came round about me daily like water: and compassed me together on every side' (v. 17) and then of the desertion by loved ones, 'My lovers and friends hast thou put away from me : and hid mine acquaintance out of my sight' (v. 18). On this same subject of disaster set in biblical terms, consider also the last paragraphs of chapter 26 of *Jane Eyre*.

Lucy, however, does find joy sometimes. Here is one such occasion.

30

Yes : I held in my hand not a slight note, but an envelope, which must, at least, contain a sheet : it felt not flimsy, but firm, substantial, satisfying. And here was the direction, 'Miss Lucy Snowe,' in a clean, clear, equal, decided hand; and here was the seal, round, full, deftly dropped by untremulous fingers, stamped with the well-cut impress of initials, 'J. G. B.' I experienced a happy feeling—a glad emotion which went warm to my heart, and ran lively through all my veins. For once a hope was realised. I held in my hand a morsel of real solid joy : not a dream, not an image of the brain, not one of those shadowy chances imagination pictures, and on which humanity starves but cannot live; not a mess of that manna I drearily eulogised a while ago—which, indeed, at first melts on the lips with an unspeakable and preter-natural sweetness, but which, in the end, our souls full surely loathe; longing deliriously for natural and earth-grown food, wildly praying Heaven's Spirits to reclaim their own spirit-dew and essence—an aliment divine, but for mortals deadly. It was neither sweet hail nor small coriander-seed—neither slight wafer, nor luscious honey, I had lighted on; it was the wild, savoury mess of the hunter, nourishing and salubrious meat, forest-fed or desert-reared, fresh, healthful, and life-sustaining. It was what the old dying patriarch demanded of his son Esau, promising in requital the blessing of his last breath. It was a godsend; and I inwardly thanked the God who had vouchsafed it. Outwardly I only thanked man, crying, 'Thank you, thank you, monsieur !'

Villette, ch. 21

Even here, however, the rarity of joy has to be emphasised ('For *once* a hope was realised'). This 'real solid joy' is
further stressed by the series of negatives that follows it.
Again Charlotte Brontë enriches the narrative by biblical
reference. The manna was heavenly food, but one can get
tired even of that, because mortals need mortals' food. The
detail of the passages describing the manna is effectively
drawn upon (see Exodus XIV, verses 14–21, 31; Numbers
XI, verses 6–9; Joshua V, verse 12). The mortals' food, 'the
wild savoury mess of the hunter', is also described in
biblical terms. The 'old dying patriarch' is Isaac, asking
Esau but, in fact, being deceitfully supplied by Jacob (see
Genesis XXVII). Isaac did not really get what he thought
he got, and Esau missed the blessing. In this reference there
is thus a final irony, for though there is temporary delight
for Lucy, it is neither genuine nor lasting. It melts away as
the manna did.

With Lucy's later history we need not here be concerned,
for it is the tale of her strange love-affair with M. Paul
Emanuel, to which sufficient reference has been made
above. We may now turn to the twin-heroines of *Shirley*,
for though the book takes its title from the more dominant
of the two, it gives us the stories of both. Like Lucy and
Jane, the first of these, Caroline Helstone, is a compara-
tively passive character, and in many ways she was a much
easier problem for Charlotte Brontë than the more assertive
Shirley, especially in relation to their love-experience. There
were, however, other facets of the problem. For one thing,
as I have said in talking about the novel's structure, there
were much broader and more varied areas of interest here
than elsewhere. In addition, by adopting the omniscient
narrator point of view, Charlotte Brontë had to consider
the men characters from a different angle whilst at the
same time she lost something of the intimacy that a heroine
telling her own story can give. Nevertheless, there is a

certain subtlety in the contrast and counter-balance of Caroline and Shirley, and this might have been yet more effective if Charlotte Brontë had known how to tell the stories of the two of them rather more concurrently and rather less successively than she does.

Amongst Shirley's early impressions of Caroline is that 'she was quiet, retiring, looked delicate, and seemed as if she needed someone to take care of her' (ch. 12). The reader does not feel that Shirley is far wrong. Much of the personal story in the first third of the novel is taken up with Caroline's apparently hopeless love for the manufacturer Robert Moore. We read this sort of internal monologue:

31

'When people love, the next step is they marry,' was her argument. 'Now, I love Robert, and I feel sure that Robert loves me: I have thought so many a time before; to-day I *felt* it. When I looked up at him after repeating Chénier's poem, his eyes (what handsome eyes he has!) sent the truth through my heart. Sometimes I am afraid to speak to him, lest I should be too frank, lest I should seem forward: for I have more than once regretted bitterly, overflowing, superfluous words, and feared I had said more than he expected me to say, and that he would disapprove what he might deem my indiscretion; now, to-night, I could have ventured to express any thought, he was so indulgent. How kind he was, as we walked up the lane! He does not flatter or say foolish things; his love-making (friendship, I mean: of course I don't yet account him my lover, but I hope he will be some day) is not like what we read of in books—it is far better—original, quiet, manly, sincere. I *do* like him: I would be an excellent wife to him if he did marry me: I would tell him of his faults (for he has a few faults), but I would study his comfort, and cherish him, and do my best to make him happy. Now, I am sure he will not be cold to-morrow: I feel almost certain that to-morrow evening he will either come here, or ask me to go there.'

Shirley, ch. 7

There is much here to suggest the overheated expectations of a rather immature girl—the argument from her own feelings, the magnification of the small incident, the hesitancy and yet the simultaneous confidence, the apologies for Robert's lack of demonstrativeness, the dreaming of the future, the final attempt at self-conviction. But he *is* cold on the morrow.

The next phase, and a long one, for Caroline is that of pessimism. At one stage it is:

'I shall not be married, it appears,' she continued. 'I suppose, as Robert does not care for me, I shall never have a husband to love nor little children to take care of.'

Shirley, ch. 10

After the belated appearance of Shirley it does not take Caroline long to decide that Shirley and Robert will marry. First, however, let us consider the description of Shirley:

32

Shirley Keeldar was no ugly heiress: she was agreeable to the eye. Her height and shape were not unlike Miss Helstone's: perhaps in stature she might have the advantage by an inch or two; she was gracefully made, and her face, too, possessed a charm as well described by the word grace as any other. It was pale naturally, but intelligent, and of varied expression. She was not a blonde, like Caroline: clear and dark were the characteristics of her aspect as to colour: her face and brow were clear, her eyes of the darkest grey: no green lights in them,—transparent, pure, natural grey: and her hair of the darkest brown. Her features were distinguished; by which I do not mean that they were high, bony, and Roman, being indeed rather small and slightly

78

marked than otherwise; but only that they were, to use a few French words, 'fins, gravieux, spirituels:' mobile they were and speaking; but their changes were not to be understood, nor their language interpreted all at once.

Shirley, ch. 11

It is worthwhile to compare this description with that of Blanche Ingram's (see Extract 21 above). One can trace the differing degrees of sympathy. The account of Blanche begins with a list of her physical attributes which reads like a catalogue. She is a thing, whereas the personality of Shirley is stressed from the very first by the reference to her name. That is followed by comment not on what she is as a piece of physique but on the effect she creates—'agreeable to the eye'. When she reaches physical attributes, Charlotte Brontë stresses the qualities of mind and character which they reflect; 'grace' is an important repeated word in the passage. There are important fine shades of difference: Blanche Ingram's features are 'noble', but those of Shirley are 'distinguished'. Against this there is a bold contrast of appearance. Blanche is striking with her black hair, white dress and amber scarf and flower, but it is clear that she aims for effect, that she is artificial. Shirley also has contrast, but it is more natural, it is not black and white but 'clear and dark'. Above all, there is the contrast between Blanche and Shirley of the statuesque and the vital. Shirley is alive. Caroline feels that all hope for herself is gone.

33

'Of course I know he will marry Shirley,' were her first words when she rose in the morning. 'And he ought to marry her: she can help him,' she added firmly. 'But I shall be forgotten when they *are* married,' was the cruel succeeding thought. 'Oh! I shall be wholly forgotten! And what—*what* shall I do when Robert is taken quite from me? Where shall I turn? *My* Robert I wish I could justly call him mine: but I am poverty and incapacity; Shirley is wealth and power: and she is beauty too, and love—I cannot deny it. This is no sordid suit: she loves him—not with inferior feelings: she loves, or *will* love, as he must feel proud to be loved. Not a valid objection can be made. Let them be married then: but afterwards I shall be nothing to him. As for being his sister, and all that stuff, I despise it. I will either be all or nothing to a man like Robert: no feeble shuffling, or false cant is endurable. Once let that pair be united, and I will certainly leave them. As for lingering about, playing the hypocrite, and pretending to calm sentiments of friendship, when my soul will be wrung with other feelings, I shall not descend to such degradation. As little could I fill the place of their mutual friend as that of their deadly foe: as little could I stand between them as trample over them. Robert is a first-rate man—in my eyes: I *have* loved, *do* love, and *must* love him. I would be his wife, if I could; as I cannot, I must go where I shall never see him. There is but one alternative—to cleave to him as if I were a part of him, or to be sundered from him as the two poles of a sphere. Sunder me then, Providence. Part us speedily.'

Shirley, ch. 14

There is a certain vigour here, as, for instance, in the spirit with which she rejects the idea of platonic friendship ('As for being his sister, and all that stuff, I despise it'), and there is also some clear-sightedness which, however, will prove in the end to have been nothing of the sort. The difficulty with Caroline, and this is by no means the worst instance of it, derives from a certain self-consciousness. Her immaturity makes this appropriate in some degree, but it also has the effect of making her statements, and particularly her passages of internal monologue, seem somewhat stilted at times.

After this passage the love of Caroline for Robert is

largely forgotten in favour of other things, and it is not until the last chapters of the novel that we find much even of Shirley's love-affairs. In a sense, Charlotte Brontë was wise to practise such economy, for Shirley is both active and forceful, 'not a manlike woman at all—not an Amazon, and yet lifting her head above both help and sympathy'. As such, it must have been more difficult for a Victorian author, and particularly a woman, to produce convincing love-scenes for someone like Shirley than for authors in almost any other period.

Time and place

One of the first things that a good novel establishes is the sense of atmosphere, and in this the suggestion of time and place plays a large part. *Shirley* is the only one of Charlotte Brontë's novels which deals either with public events or with a period markedly outside her own time. In this novel she is quick to tell us that 'We are going back to the beginning of this century' (ch. 1). This assertion she substantiates by contrasting her curates and their ways with those that she alleges would be found at the time of the novel's publication in 1850. The more precise dating (1811–12) is mentioned, but its particular relevance does not appear until later when reference is made to the Orders in Council issued by Britain as part of her strategy of economic warfare against Napoleon in 1807. In two paragraphs Charlotte Brontë provides a succinct description of the state of affairs.

34

The period of which I write was an overshadowed one in British history, and especially in the history of the northern provinces. War was then at its height. Europe was all involved therein. England, if not weary, was worn with long resistance: yes, and half her people were weary too, and cried out for peace on any terms. National honour was become a mere empty name, of no value in the eyes of many, because their sight was dim with famine; and for a morsel of meat they would have sold their birthright.

The 'Orders in Council,' provoked by Napoleon's Milan and Berlin decrees, and forbidding neutral powers to trade with France, had, by offending America, cut off the principal market of the Yorkshire woollen trade, and brought it consequently to the verge of ruin. Minor foreign markets were glutted, and would receive no more: the Brazils, Portugal, Sicily were all overstocked by nearly two years' consumption. At this crisis, certain inventions in machinery were introduced into the staple manufactures of the north, which, greatly reducing the number of hands necessary to be employed, threw thousands out of work, and left them without legitimate means of sustaining life. A bad harvest supervened. Distress reached its climax. Endurance, over-goaded, stretched the hand of fraternity to sedition. The throes of a sort of moral earthquake were felt heaving under the hills of the northern counties. But, as is usual in such cases, nobody took much notice. When a food-riot broke out in a manufacturing town, when a gig-mill was burnt to the ground, or a manufacturer's house was attacked, the furniture thrown into the streets, and the family forced to flee for their lives, some local measures were or were not taken by the local magistracy; a ringleader was detected, or more frequently suffered to elude detection; newspaper paragraphs were written on the subject, and there the thing stopped. As to the sufferers, whose sole inheritance was labour, and who had lost that inheritance—who could not get work, and consequently could not get wages, and consequently could not get bread—they were left to suffer on; perhaps inevitably left: it would not do to stop the progress of invention, to damage science by discouraging its improvements; the war could not be terminated, efficient relief could not be raised: there was no help then; so the unemployed underwent their destiny—ate the bread and drank the waters of affliction.

Shirley, ch. 2

This passage is a masterpiece of lucid summary, skilfully listing the events and relating them to their human consequences. Charlotte Brontë aptly turns at the completion of her account of events, ending with the bad harvest, to the effects. On the short sentence 'Distress reached its climax' the passage moves to the 'moral earthquake'. This image has been preceded by a sentence that looks flat but yet is pregnant with significance—the turning of 'fraternity to sedition', the 'overgoading' of endurance. We then get vivid detail of local incident, and the passage ends with an ambiguous, perhaps puzzled, but also very sympathetic statement of what happened to the victims of the machinery revolution in textiles ('As to the sufferers . . . they were left to suffer on . . . [they] ate the bread and drank the waters of affliction'). Notice the easily recurring biblical allusion once again.

Events in *Shirley* go on from there, and likewise in *Villette* they follow a straightforward chronological course. This is also largely the case with *Jane Eyre*, and neither here nor in *Villette* is there need of a historical setting. *Jane Eyre*, however, does need retrospect, and thus we hear something of Jane's family past both during her visit to the Reeds in the middle of the novel and, of course, when St. John Rivers has to inform her of her inheritance. More important still is Rochester's past, and thus we have the occasions on which he (and he alone can do it) tells of his life with his mistresses and of his first marriage. One passage from his description of this latter is worth quoting for its intensity of description.

35

'One night I had been awakened by her yells—(since the medical men had pronounced her mad, she had, of course, been shut up)—it was a fiery West Indian night; one of the description that frequently precede the hurricanes of those climates. Being unable to sleep in bed, I got up and opened the window. The air was like sulphur-streams—I could find no refreshment anywhere. Mosquitoes came buzzing in and hummed sullenly round the room; the sea, which I could hear from thence, rumbled dull like an earthquake—black clouds were casting up over it; the moon was setting in the waves, broad and red, like a hot cannon-ball—she threw her last bloody glance over a world quivering with the ferment of tempest. I was physically influenced by the atmosphere and scene, and my ears were filled with the curses the maniac still shrieked out; wherein she momentarily mingled my name with such a tone of demon-hate, with such language!—no professed harlot ever had a fouler vocabulary than she: though two rooms off, I heard every word—the thin partitions of the West Indian house opposing but slight obstruction to her wolfish cries.

'"This life", said I at last, "is hell: this is the air—those are the sounds of the bottomless pit! I have a right to deliver myself from it if I can. The sufferings of this mortal state will have me with the heavy flesh that now cumbers my soul. Of the fanatic's burning eternity I have no fear: there is not a future state worse than this present one—let me break away, and go home to God!"'

Jane Eyre, ch. 27

This indeed is 'a world quivering with the ferment of tempest'; it is a world that belongs to madness; it is Rochester's 'hell'.

In the period of her happiness with Rochester Jane Eyre exclaims: 'I wondered why moralists call this world a

85

dreary wilderness; for me it blossomed like a rose' (ch. 25).
In fact, this is but testimony to the way in which Charlotte
Brontë often makes external circumstance (and especially
seasons) correspond to Jane's feelings. Thus as she contemplates the departure to Lowood School, unpleasant as her
aunt's home had been, she is desolate in a desolate scene.

36

I opened the glass-door in the breakfast-room: the shrub-
bery was quite still: the black frost reigned, unbroken by
sun or breeze, through the grounds. I covered my head and
arms with the skirt of my frock, and went out to walk in
a part of the plantation which was quite sequestered; but
I found no pleasure in the silent trees, the falling fir-cones,
the congealed relics of autumn, russet leaves swept by past
winds in heaps, and now stiffened together. I leaned against
a gate, and looked into an empty field where no sheep were
feeding, where the short grass was nipped and blanched.
It was a very gray day; a most opaque sky, 'onding on
snaw', canopied all; then flakes fell at intervals, which
settled on the hard path and on the hoary lea without melt-
ing. I stood, a wretched child enough, whispering to myself
over and over again, 'What shall I do?—what shall I do?'

Jane Eyre, ch. 4

It is winter, a time of 'black frost', all is still ('silent
trees', 'congealed relics', leaves 'stiffened together'), all is
vacant ('empty field', 'no sheep'), all is gray. It was an appropriate season to go from one bad place to another, and at
Lowood 'now, at the latter end of January, all was wintry
blight and brown decay . . . all under foot was still soak-
ing wet with the floods of yesterday' (ch. 5). But Jane learns
to endure, and her more settled condition corresponds with
winter's giving way to spring.

Midsummer is, indeed could only be, synonymous with
happiness at Thornfield.

A splendid Midsummer shone over England: skies so pure, suns so radiant as were then seen in long succession, seldom favour, even singly, our wave-girt land. It was as if a band of Italian days had come from the South, like a flock of glorious passenger birds, and lighted to rest them on the cliffs of Albion. The hay was all got in; the fields round Thornfield were green and shorn; the roads white and baked; the trees were in their dark prime; hedge and wood, full-leaved and deeply tinted, contrasted well with the sunny hue of the cleared meadows between.

Jane Eyre, ch. 23

It is an idyllic setting down to its last detail.

I went apart into the orchard. No nook in the grounds more sheltered and more Eden-like; a very high wall shut it out from the court on one side; on the other a beech avenue screened it from the lawn. At the bottom was a sunk fence, its sole separation from lonely fields: a winding walk, bordered with laurels and terminating in a giant horse-chestnut, circled at the base by a seat, led down to the fence.

ibid.

That 'giant horse-chestnut' is important, for this is the scene of Rochester's proposal of marriage to Jane, immediately after which we read:

But what had befallen the night? The moon was not yet set, and we were all in shadow. I could scarcely see my master's face, near as I was. And what ailed the chestnut tree?—it writhed and groaned; while wind roared in the laurel walk, and came sweeping over us.

ibid.

The chapter ends with the paragraph:

Before I left my bed in the morning, little Adèle came

running in to tell me that the great horse-chestnut at the bottom of the orchard had been struck by lightning in the night, and half of it split away.

ibid.

And on the night before the 'marriage' there is a storm.

It was not without a certain wild pleasure I ran before the wind, delivering my trouble of mind to the measureless air-torrent thundering through space. Descending the laurel walk, I faced the wreck of the chestnut-tree; it stood up, black and riven: the trunk, split down the centre, gasped ghastly. The cloven halves were not broken from each other, for the firm base and strong roots kept them unsundered below; though community of vitality was destroyed —the sap could flow no more: their great boughs on each side were dead, and next winter's tempests would be sure to fell one or both to earth: as yet, however, they might be said to form one tree—a ruin, but an entire ruin.

Jane Eyre, ch. 25

It does not require emphasis upon the effects of nature, upon their symbolic interference.

These passages show too that place, as well as time, can have a symbolic importance. Rochester, in fact, compares himself in his mutilated condition at the end to 'the old lightning-struck chestnut-tree in Thornfield orchard'. The link of place and character is used explicitly for purposes of contrast in *Shirley*. Charlotte Brontë asks: 'How did [the summer] lapse with Shirley and Caroline? Let us first visit the heiress.' Here is part of the answer:

38

She keeps her dark old manor-house light and bright with her cheery presence: the gallery, and the low-ceiled chambers that open into it, have learned lively echoes from her voice: the dim entrance-hall, with its one window, has grown pleasantly accustomed to the frequent rustle of a silk dress, as its wearer sweeps across from room to room, now carrying flowers to the barbarous peach-bloom salon, now entering the dining-room to open its casements and let in the scent of mignonette and sweetbriar, anon bringing plants from the staircase-window to place in the sun at the open porch-door.

Shirley, ch. 22

By contrast, this is Caroline's lot:

Caroline was limited once more to the gray Rectory; the solitary morning walk in remote bypaths; the long, lonely afternoon sitting in a quiet parlour which the sun forsook at noon, or in the garden alcove where it shone bright, yet sad, on the ripening red currants trained over the trellis, and on the fair monthly roses entwined between, and through them fell chequered on Caroline sitting in her white summer dress, still as a garden statue. There she read old books, taken from her uncle's library.

ibid.

At Fieldhead Shirley is gay, she has even compelled the gloom of the old manor-house to take on her gaiety with its new lightness and its summer flowers. At the Rectory the gloom abides. Gray, solitary, remote, long, lonely, quiet, sad, still, old—these are the adjectives.

In these passages place underlines mood. Elsewhere, as for instance in the description of the red-room at Gateshead, place itself becomes oppressive. As the scene of Jane's imprisonment the red-room itself becomes hateful, an instrument of her suffering.

39

The red-room was a spare chamber, very seldom slept in: I might say never, indeed, unless when a chance influx of

CB—G

visitors at Gateshead Hall rendered it necessary to turn to account all the accommodation it contained: yet it was one of the largest and stateliest chambers in the mansion. A bed supported on massive pillars of mahogany, hung with curtains of deep red damask, stood out like a tabernacle in the centre, the two large windows, with their blinds always drawn down, were half shrouded in festoons and falls of similar drapery; the carpet was red; the table at the foot of the bed was covered with a crimson cloth; the walls were a soft fawn colour, with a blush of pink in it; the wardrobe, the toilet-table, the chairs, were of darkly-polished old mahogany. Out of these deep surroundings shades rose high, and glared white, the piled-up mattresses and pillows of the bed, spread with a snowy Marseilles counterpane. Scarcely less prominent was an ample cushioned easy-chair near the head of the bed, also white, with a footstool before it, and looking, as I thought, like a pale throne.

This room was chill, because it seldom had a fire; it was silent, because remote from the nursery and kitchens; solemn, because it was known to be so seldom entered. The housemaid alone came here on Saturdays, to wipe from the mirrors and the furniture a week's quiet dust; and Mrs. Reed herself, at far intervals, visited it to review the contents of a certain secret drawer in the wardrobe, where were stored divers parchments, her jewel-casket, and a miniature of her deceased husband; and in those last words lies the secret of the red-room—the spell which kept it so lonely in spite of its grandeur.

Mr. Reed had been dead nine years: it was in this chamber he breathed his last; here he lay in state; hence his coffin was borne by the undertaker's men; and, since that day, a sense of dreary consecration had guarded it from frequent intrusion.

Jane Eyre, ch. 2

This passage begins with colour, with accumulating and oppressive red everywhere, except for the stark contrasts of white bed-linen. It is a vast room ('one of the largest'; the bed has 'massive pillars'; 'two large windows'; 'the piled-up mattresses' are high; even the easy-chair is 'ample'), especially to a child. The visual effect is accompanied by similar tactile and auditory effects—chill and silent. Finally, and as a climax, there are the associations of death, giving it overall 'a sense of dreary consecration' and making it much like a horrifying mausoleum. Rich as it was in biblical allusion, Charlotte Brontë's memory deftly brings forth an apt reference to the 'pale throne', recalling the great white throne in Revelation XX, 11, before which the judgment of the dead takes place—just one more constituent of the frightening scene for the little child.

Much the most important of Charlotte Brontë's locations is Thornfield, the home of Rochester. Mention has already been made of the use Charlotte Brontë makes of certain areas of it, but the hall in itself has a continuing significance. Here is Jane's first view of its front.

40

Advancing on to the lawn, I looked up and surveyed the front of the mansion. It was three stories high, of proportions not vast, though considerable; a gentleman's manor-house, not a nobleman's seat: battlements round the top gave it a picturesque look. Its gray front stood out well from the background of a rookery, whose cawing tenants were now on the wing. They flew over the lawn and grounds to alight in a great meadow, from which these were separated by a sunk fence, and where an array of mighty old thorn trees, strong, knotty, and broad as oaks, at once explained the etymology of the mansion's designation.

Jane Eyre, ch. 11

There is nothing singular, because there is nothing meant to be; it is 'a gentleman's manor-house'. It is exactly right and pleasing. Later, before her 'marriage', Jane dreams about Thornfield.

41

'I dreamt another dream, sir: that Thornfield Hall was a dreary ruin, the retreat of bats and owls. I thought that of all the stately front nothing remained but a shell-like wall. very high and very fragile-looking. I wandered, on a moon-light night, through the grass-grown enclosure within: here I stumbled over a marble hearth, and there over a fallen fragment of cornice.   *Jane Eyre*, ch. 25

There is more, much more than this personal detail; for instance, we hear of the fleeing of Rochester, the unknown child and the vampire-woman. But for our present purposes this is enough, for it serves to show the prophetic purpose of the dream fulfilled in the ultimate reality at the end.

42

I looked with timorous joy towards a stately house; I saw a blackened ruin.

No need to cower behind a gatepost, indeed!—to peep up at chamber lattices, fearing life was astir behind them! No need to listen for doors opening—to fancy steps on the pavements or the gravel walk! The lawn, the grounds were trodden and waste: the portal yawned void. The front was, as I had once seen it in a dream, but a shell-like wall, very high and very fragile-looking, perforated with paneless windows: no roof, no battlements, no chimneys—all had crashed in.   *Jane Eyre*, ch. 36

Thornfield is noble but cursed, like the love of Rochester and Jane. Its fortunes parallel theirs.

Here is a further reminder that Charlotte Brontë rarely described place, and time almost never, for its own sake. The accounts either reflect or affect the characters. They serve, that is, for the most part, to tell us not what place or time is like, but rather of the way the characters react to their environment.

Speech

An author may describe event and character, place and time, but his ultimate success will depend upon the dramatic as much as, and probably more than, upon the narrated, upon the directly rather than the indirectly represented. The way to be direct is to let the characters speak for themselves, preferably in dialogue but, failing that, in internal monologue (i.e. expressing their own thoughts to themselves).

In those novels where the central character tells his or her own story the scope for knowing exactly what internal monologue goes on is restricted to the narrator. Because this character can go fully in upon herself, the novelist derives a certain strength, especially in passages of isolation and prolonged stress. Examples of internal monologue in *Jane Eyre* have been analysed above (see pp. 65–6), but Charlotte Brontë also used internal monologue for at least one character where, technically speaking, there was not the same necessity, in *Shirley*. That character is Caroline (see pp. 77–8), for whom this device was particularly appropriate in her quiet, introspective condition with her feelings of isolation, as she thought that the two most close to her, Robert Moore and Shirley, the two to whom she might have confided her troubles, were unapproachable. One example of this monologue must be quoted, for in its emotional intensity it rises almost to frenzy.

43

'Oh! I *should* see him once more before all is over: Heaven *might* favour me thus far!' she cried. 'God grant me a little comfort before I die!' was her humble petition.

'But he will not know I am ill till I am gone; and he will come when they have laid me out, and I am senseless, cold, and stiff.

'What can my departed soul feel then? Can it see or know what happens to the clay? Can spirits, through any medium, communicate with living flesh? Can the dead at all revisit those they leave? Can they come in the elements? Will wind, water, fire, lend me a path to Moore?

'Is it for nothing the wind sounds almost articulately sometimes—sings as I have lately heard it sing at night—or passes the casement sobbing, as if for sorrow to come? Does nothing, then, haunt it—nothing inspire it? . . .

'What is that electricity they speak of, whose changes make us well or ill: whose lack or excess blasts; whose even balance revives? . . .

'*Where* is the other world? In *what* will another life consist? Why do I ask? Have I not cause to think that the hour is hasting but too fast when the veil must be rent for me? Do I not know the Grand Mystery is likely to burst prematurely on me? Great Spirit! in whose goodness I confide; whom, as my Father, I have petitioned night and morning from early infancy, help the weak creation of thy hands! Sustain me through the ordeal I dread and must undergo! Give me strength! Give me patience! Give me— oh! *give me* FAITH!'

Shirley, ch. 24

One notices the insistent questioning, the at times apparently irrational drifting from subject to subject, the obsession with the more than sensory, the characteristically Brontëan religious element, the final desperate petition.

Generally, however, dialogue is the only direct means available for revealing the thoughts and feelings of characters other than the narrator. Even in the early novel *The Professor* Charlotte Brontë shows a well-developed talent for conversation. Yet though dialogue plays quite a large part in *The Professor*, there are occasions when the reader feels that opportunities have been missed. For example, after speaking of the way in which he with 'the sardonic disdain of a fortuneless subordinate' has impressed the proprietress of the school in which he teaches more than Monsieur Pelet with his 'most flattering assiduities of a prosperous chef d'institution', Crimsworth goes on to narrate:

44

Next day, when I saw the directress, and when she made an excuse to meet me in the corridor, and besought my notice by a demeanour and look subdued to Helot humility, I could not love, I could scarcely pity her. To answer briefly and dryly some interesting inquiry about my health —to pass her by with a stern bow—was all I could.

The Professor, ch. 20

Dramatic effect is lost in exclusive report.
Contrast this passage from *Jane Eyre*.

45

'No sight so sad as that of a naughty child,' he began, 'especially a naughty little girl. Do you know where the wicked go after death?'

'They go to hell,' was my ready and orthodox answer.

'And what is hell? Can you tell me that?'

'A pit full of fire.'

'And should you like to fall into that pit, and to be there burning for ever?'

'No, sir.'

'What must you do to avoid it?'

I deliberated a moment; my answer, when it did come, was objectionable: 'I must keep in good health and not die.'

Jane Eyre, ch. 4

Mr. Brocklehurst tries condescension, mingled with instruction, and reproof. Jane is more than a match for both of these. The reader readily appreciates the humour that instantly explodes the carefully-prepared climax of Brocklehurst's cross-examination, after the previous answers, so 'ready and orthodox', seemed to suggest that success was inevitable.

Charlotte Brontë can often reveal character most economically through dialogue, as, for example, in this conversation between the parson Helstone and his niece Caroline in *Shirley*.

46

'Uncle,' said she, 'whenever you speak of marriage you speak of it scornfully. Do you think people shouldn't marry?'

'It is decidedly the wisest plan to remain single, especially for women.'

'Are all marriages unhappy?'

'Millions of marriages are unhappy. If everybody confessed the truth, perhaps all are more or less so.'

'You are always vexed when you are asked to come and marry a couple. Why?'

'Because one does not like to act as accessory to the commission of a piece of pure folly.' . . .

'But you have been married. Why were you so inconsistent as to marry?'

'Every man is mad once or twice in his life.'

Shirley, ch. 7

A guide word is given at the beginning of this passage in the adverb 'scornfully' and we are meant to build upon that. Notice how the passage gradually increases the acerbity of Helstone's replies. These proceed from maxim to generalisation to satire to bitterness.

In a passage of convincing dialect (and this does not necessarily mean accurate to the last linguistic detail) Charlotte Brontë makes the workman William Farrar distinguish types of pride. He is speaking with Caroline and Shirley.

47

'Ay, I *am* proud, and so are ye; but your pride and mine is t' raight mak'—what we call i' Yorkshire clean pride—such as Mr. Malone and Mr. Donne knows nought about. Theirs is mucky pride. . . .'

'What is the difference, William?'

'Ye know t' difference weel enow, but ye want me to get a gate o' talking. Mr. Malone and Mr. Donne is almost too proud to do aught for theirsel'n; *we* are almost too proud to let anybody do aught for us. T' curates can hardly bide to speak a civil word to them they think beneath them; *we* can hardly bide to tak' an uncivil word fro' them that thinks themsel'n aboon us.'

Shirley, ch. 18

This passage shows clearly that dialogue can reveal information about at least three people, namely, the person speaking, the person addressed and the person(s) spoken about. It is, of course, usually the last about whom the information is apparently clearest, but it can only be apparently, because, as in life, we bring outside criteria to judge whether we should accept what is said. And this will include what we already know of those spoken about. Here our knowledge of Malone and Donne disposes us to believe William Farrar, and so does the trust which Caroline and

Shirley place in him. The use of dialect in this passage provides not only a sense of authenticity but adds to our feeling about Farrar's basic honesty and reliability.

To see Charlotte Brontë's range, compare this passage with the serious moral conversation of Rochester reflecting on his way of life to Jane Eyre.

48

'Dread remorse when you are tempted to err, Miss Eyre: remorse is the poison of life.'

'Repentance is said to be its cure, sir.'

'It is not its cure. Reformation may be its cure; and I could reform—I have strength yet for that—if—but where is the use of thinking of it, hampered, burdened, cursed as I am? Besides, since happiness is irrevocably denied me, I have a right to get pleasure out of life: and I *will* get it, cost what it may.'

'Then you will degenerate still more, sir.'

'Possibly: yet why should I, if I can get sweet, fresh pleasure? And I may get it as sweet and fresh as the wild honey the bee gathers on the moor.'

'It will sting—it will taste bitter, sir.'

'How do you know?—you never tried it. How very serious—how very solemn you look; and you are as ignorant of the matter as this cameo head' (taking one from the mantelpiece). 'You have no right to preach to me, you neophyte, that have not passed the porch of life, and are absolutely unacquainted with its mysteries.'

'I only remind you of your own words, sir: you said error brought remorse, and you pronounced remorse the poison of existence.'

'And who talks of error now? I scarcely think the notion that flitted across my brain was an error. I believe it was an inspiration rather than a temptation: it was very genial, very soothing—I know that. Here it comes again! It is no devil, I assure you; or if it be, it has put on the robes of an angel of light. I think I must admit so fair a guest when it asks entrance to my heart.'

Jane Eyre, ch. 14

The tone is solemn, but in Jane it is much more simple than in Rochester. Compare the plainness of her sentences with his. Not only are his more involved, they are also more varied and sometimes more disjointed. He, of course, is moved by 'the notion that flittered across [his] brain', but Jane is unaware of what that is.

Dialogue finds its most important use in incidents of high emotion. Here Jane has resolved to leave Thornfield. Rochester speaks:

49

'Come to my side, Jane, and let us explain and understand one another.'

'I will never again come to your side: I am torn away now, and cannot return.'

'But, Jane, I summon you as my wife: it is you only I intend to marry.'

I was silent: I thought he mocked me.

'Come, Jane—come hither.'

'Your bride stands between us.'

He rose, and with a stride reached me.

'My bride is here,' he said, again drawing me to him, 'because my equal is here, and my likeness. Jane, will you marry me?'

Still I did not answer, and still I writhed myself from his grasp: for I was still incredulous.

'Do you doubt me, Jane?'

'Entirely.'

'You have no faith in me?'

'Not a whit.'

'Am I a liar in your eyes?' he asked passionately. 'Little sceptic, you *shall* be convinced. What love have I for Miss Ingram? None: and that you know. What love has she for me? None: as I have taken pains to prove: . . . I love you as my own flesh. You—poor and obscure, and small and plain as you are—I entreat to accept me as a husband.'

'What, me!' I ejaculated, beginning in his earnestness—and especially in his incivility—to credit his sincerity: 'me who have not a friend in the world but you—if you are my friend: not a shilling but what you have given me?'

'You, Jane, I must have you for my own—entirely my own. Will you be mine? Say yes, quickly.'

'Mr. Rochester, let me look at your face: turn to the moonlight.'

'Why?'

'Because I want to read your countenance—turn!'

'There! you will find it scarcely more legible than a crumpled, scratched page. Read on: only make haste, for I suffer.'

His face was very much agitated and very much flushed, and there were strong workings in the features, and strange gleams in the eyes.

'Oh, Jane, you torture me!' he exclaimed. 'With that searching and yet faithful and generous look, you torture me!'

'How can I do that? If you are true, and your offer real, my only feelings to you must be gratitude and devotion—they cannot torture.'

'Gratitude!' he ejaculated; and added wildly—'Jane, accept me quickly. Say, Edward—give me my name—Edward—I will marry you.'

'Are you in earnest? Do you truly love me? Do you sincerely wish me to be your wife?'

'I do; and if an oath is necessary to satisfy, I swear it.'

'Then, sir, I will marry you.'

'Edward—my little wife!'

'Dear Edward!'

Jane Eyre, ch. 23

As good dialogue of high drama should be, this is short, rapid, economical, moving the state of emotion with every speech, yet moving on each occasion with varied pace and direction. It is cleverly linked also with the gestures and attitudes of the two characters and admirably brings out the depth of feeling involved.

Narrative standpoint

Much has been said about the consequences of having a first-person hero(ine) narrator, but one or two more observations need to be made.

There are the obvious advantages of the fullest direct revelation for the most important character, but there are also two serious disadvantages. We are not allowed to see as much as we might of the heroine as others see her, and we only see the others either as she sees them or as they tell about themselves to her. This means that they some-times have to tell a lot about their pasts. Unsatisfactory though in many ways they are, this at least is one of the virtues of the opening chapters of *Villette*, that they tell us not only about Lucy's early years but also about John Bretton's and the Bretton household generally.

No such convenient situation is available to Rochester, and thus he has to tell about his wife and his mistresses. That past mars and nearly destroys his (and Jane's) present. To Charlotte Brontë's credit be it said that it is very strategically situated. We have the mysterious cries and the terrifying acts and these are bad enough, but then comes the attempt at bigamy and the revelation of the existence of the mad wife. Everything, narratively speaking, falls into place, but it is perhaps more important that Rochester has by now become such a sympathetic character that we accept his explanation without question.

50

'I must be provided for by a wealthy marriage. [My father] sought me a partner betimes. Mr. Mason, a West India planter and merchant, was his old acquaintance. He was certain his possessions were real and vast : he made inquiries. Mr. Mason, he found, had a son and daughter; and he learned from him that he could and would give the latter a fortune of thirty thousand pounds : that sufficed. When I left college, I was sent out to Jamaica, to espouse a bride already courted for me. My father said nothing about her money; but he told me Miss Mason was the boast of Spanish Town for her beauty : and this was no lie. I found her a fine woman, in the style of Blanche Ingram : tall, dark, and majestic. Her family wished to secure me, because I was of a good race; and so did she. They showed her to me in parties splendidly dressed. I seldom saw her alone, and had very little private conversation with her. She flattered me, and lavishly displayed for my pleasure her charms and accomplishments. All the men in her circle seemed to admire her and envy me. I was dazzled, stimulated : my senses were excited; and being ignorant, raw and inexperienced, I thought I loved her. There is no folly so besotted that the idiotic rivalries of society, the prurience, the rashness, the blindness of youth, will not hurry a man to its commission. Her relatives encouraged me : competitors piqued me : she allured me : a marriage was achieved almost before I knew where I was. Oh, I have no respect for myself when I think of that act!—an agony of inward contempt masters me. I never loved, I never esteemed, I did not even know her. I was not sure of the existence of one virtue in her nature : I had marked neither modesty nor benevolence, nor candour, nor refinement in her mind or manners—and, I married

her: gross, grovelling, mole-eyed blockhead that I was!'
Jane Eyre, ch. 27

Notice how much is made of Rochester's helplessness in the whole matter, of his father's arrangements, the Masons' scheming and parading him around, their encouragement, his wife's flattery, his own ignorance and immaturity, the general sense of being rushed into something whose importance he just did not realise. In the onrush of description, explanation and apology we are never given a moment to question.

Authorial viewpoint

Charlotte Brontë's narrative method does not, except in *Shirley*, offer her much direct opportunity to express her own views, and even in that novel she relates those views quite closely to what is going on. There is little that might be called gratuitous intrusion. Thus in her description of a Methodist service she quotes snatches of Wesley's hymns (all incidentally to be found in the 1876 volume except the dreadful verse

> Sleeping on the brink of sin)

and in between she describes the exclamations. It will be enough to quote one of these:

51

Here followed an interval of clamorous prayer, accompanied by fearful groans. A shout of 'I've found liberty!' 'Doad o' Bill's has fun' liberty!' rung from the chapel and out all the assembly broke again:

> What a mercy of this!
> What a heaven of bliss! . . .
>
> *Shirley*, ch. 9

There was a good deal of ecclesiastical strife in the first

half of the nineteenth century, and members of the Church of England resented the religious pretensions of ignorant men who often found influence and power among the Dissenters. The portrait of Moses Barraclough in *Shirley* is an excellent example of this animosity. In the passage quoted, however, the feeling is not so much that of animosity as of ridicule, a ridicule evoked both from the situation and from the characters. Notice the effective use made of the descent into dialect, strengthened by the local description of the man concerned first by his nickname ('Doad', probably a form of 'George') and then by the patronymic ('o' Bill's' meaning 'son of Bill').

Obviously in a clerical household the subject of ecclesiastical differences must often have arisen. It occupied Charlotte Brontë elsewhere in *Shirley*. Thus at the beginning, though the events are set in 1811–12, she devotes a paragraph to church views in 1850.

52

Of late years, I say, an abundant shower of curates has fallen upon the North of England; but in eighteen-hundred-eleven-twelve that affluent rain had not descended; . . . The present successors of the apostles, disciples of Dr. Pusey and tools of the Propaganda, were at that time being hatched under cradle-blankets, or undergoing regeneration by nursery-baptism in wash-hand-basins. You could not have guessed by looking at any one of them that the Italian-ironed double frills of its net-cap surrounded the brows of a pre-ordained, specially sanctified successor to St. Paul, St. Peter, or St. John : nor could you have seen in the folds of its long night-gown the white surplice in which it was hereafter cruelly to exercise the souls of its parishioners, and strangely to nonplus its old-fashioned vicar by flourishing aloft in a pulpit the shirt-like raiment which had never before waved higher than the reading-desk.

Shirley, ch. 1

In this passage she makes much of the contentious inno-vations brought in by the High Churchmen of the Oxford Movement. She ridicules the doctrine of baptismal regene-ration by her reference to 'nursery-baptism in wash-hand-basins'; she hits at that of apostolic succession of the clergy with the deliberately inflated reference to a 'pre-ordained, specially sanctified successor of St. Paul, St. Peter, or St. John', this list suggesting that it scarcely matters which; she equates the child's night-gown and the surplice ('shirt-like raiment'), the wearing of which to preach in as well as to read the service caused much scandal at the time.

On one religious topic, that of Roman Catholicism, her dislike was extreme. Charlotte Brontë's own strong feeling finds vent in Lucy's outbursts.

53

This book contained legends of the saints. Good God! (I speak the words reverently) what legends they were. What gasconading rascals those saints must have been, if they first boasted these exploits or invented these miracles. These legends, however, were no more than monkish extravagances, over which one laughed inwardly; there were, besides, priestly matters, and the priestcraft of the book was far worse than its monkery. The ears burned on each side of my head as I listened, perforce, to tales of moral martyrdom inflicted by Rome; the dread boasts of confessors, who had wickedly abused their office, trampling to deep degradation high-born ladies, making of countesses and princesses the most tormented slaves under the sun. Stories like that of Conrad and Elizabeth of Hungary, re-curred again and again, with all its dreadful viciousness, sickening tyranny and black impiety: tales that were night-mares of oppression, privation, and agony.

Villette, ch. 13

In this passage from *Villette* the character is expressing

the same feelings as the author expresses in her own person elsewhere. Often we can only infer the author's opinions either from the quality of the writing or from autobiographical parallels. An example of the former is the end of *Jane Eyre*, also on a religious subject, the self-sacrificing labours of St. John Rivers in the mission-field.

54

As to St. John Rivers, he left England: he went to India. He entered on the path he had marked for himself; he pursues it still. A more resolute, indefatigable pioneer never wrought amidst rocks and dangers. Firm, faithful, and devoted, full of energy and zeal, and truth, he labours for his race; he clears their painful way to improvement; he hews down like a giant the prejudices of creed and caste that encumber it. He may be stern; he may be exacting; he may be ambitious yet; but his is the sternness of the warrior Greatheart, who guards his pilgrim convoy from the onslaught of Apollyon. His is the exaction of the apostle, who speaks but for Christ, when he says, 'Whosoever will come after Me, let him deny himself, and take up his cross and follow Me.' His is the ambition of the high master-spirit, which aims to fill a place in the first rank of those who are redeemed from the earth—who stand without fault before the throne of God, who share the last mighty victories of the Lamb, who are called, and chosen, and faithful.

Jane Eyre, ch. 38

As in the critical passage from *Villette* this extract derives much of its power from its adjectives, at any rate at the beginning. Then there is the sense of struggle and determination—and success, in the closely adjoining verbs of effort ('he labours . . . he clears . . . he hews down . . .'). Again, there is the parallelism, giving force to the rhetorical structure, in 'His is the sternness . . . His is the exaction . . . His is the ambition . . .'. Then there is the comparison with the highest Christian experience first of toil and then of victory, first of cross and then of crown. By that the initial adjectives 'firm, faithful and devoted' are turned into their final form of 'called, and chosen, and faithful'. This is Charlotte Brontë expressing her own view through that of one character as that character considers another.

There is also the case where she seems simply to express through her narrator-character feelings that she herself, from our knowledge of her life, must have keenly experienced. Consider Jane Eyre's sense of frustration in the following passage.

55

It is in vain to say human beings ought to be satisfied with tranquillity : they must have action; and they will make it if they cannot find it. Millions are condemned to a stiller doom than mine, and millions are in silent revolt against their lot. Nobody knows how many rebellions besides political rebellions ferment in the masses of life which people earth. Women are supposed to be very calm gene- rally : but women feel just as men feel; they need exercise for their faculties, and a field for their efforts as much as their brothers do; they suffer from too rigid a restraint, too absolute a stagnation, precisely as men would suffer; and it is narrow-minded in their more privileged fellow-creatures to say that they ought to confine themselves to making pud- dings and knitting stockings, to playing on the piano and embroidering bags. It is thoughtless to condemn them, or laugh at them, if they seek to do more or learn more than custom has pronounced necessary for their sex.

Jane Eyre, ch. 12

This is passionate feminism. Jane becomes here the

archetypal woman, representative of all her kind in their external revolt against the restrictions placed upon them. Notice the aggrieved feeling which gives force to the expression 'But women feel just as men feel', with the subsequent accusation of masculine narrow-mindedness.

Summary

At the beginning of the nineteenth chapter of *The Professor* Charlotte Brontë writes:

Novelists should never allow themselves to be weary of the study of real life. If they observed this duty conscientiously, they would give us fewer pictures chequered with vivid contrasts of light and shade; they would seldom elevate their heroes and heroines to the heights of rapture —still seldomer sink them to the depths of despair; for if we rarely taste the fullness of joy in this life, we yet more rarely savour the acrid bitterness of hopeless anguish.

This statement may seem rather strange coming from her. 'The study of real life' hardly sits easy alongside the sensational and the neo-Gothic that is a marked feature of her work. And it is not hard to find 'vivid contrasts of light and shade' and heroines in 'the depths of despair', if not so frequently on 'the heights of rapture'. Of course, this is from her first novel, and she may be allowed to have modified her practice in her later work.

Yet there is much in this passage that is true. What is not true of Charlotte Brontë's later work is its positing a fundamental distinction between 'the study of real life' and 'vivid contrasts of light and shade'. Her heroines come from real life, and yet they have much of such contrasts. They come, as has been sufficiently stressed above, from Charlotte Brontë's own life, and by their isolation and solitariness their joys and sorrows are magnified to give just such contrasts as she develops in the latter part of the passage quoted. This is the especial value of Charlotte Brontë's explanation of experience through the lives of her heroines. These characters are ordinary in the extreme, poor, isolated, plain. The ordinariness of people like Jane Eyre and Lucy Snowe is emphasised by contrast with those who are beautiful and wealthy. They become extraordinary by their exposure to situations which bring out the elemental human experiences of suffering and love. I have emphasised the subjectivity of the novels and as a result of this the centrality of the heroines. For the most part, these are passive characters to whom things happen. They are made to suffer. But they are also isolated, unprotected characters, with no one to whom to turn. This means that their suffering is yet greater. But being isolated, they yearn for communion and sympathy; that is, they love and they love intensely.

Here we touch upon another important aspect of Charlotte Brontë's work—the relation of the sexes. Her heroines have to be independent, and they are quite capable of being so, but both they and she realise that feminine independence in a masculine world is no easy achievement. It is hemmed in by restrictions and prohibitions. Moreover, heroines of this kind cannot be satisfied by merely ordinary men. In all the three main novels there are men of outstanding sexual power as the main characters. Meeting such men acts as a catalytic experience by which life becomes at once more stimulating, more exciting, more complicated and more fearful. By this means also the ordinary is transcended to become the extraordinary. Hence the expression of this in the action—often by the horrible, by the fantastic and the sensational, by dreams and storms, vampires and apparitions. This heightening, this stretching of the characters' nerves, brings out the underlying resilience and strength, the basic heroism of ordinary women. In its turn this is seen to have its roots in the strong moral and religious beliefs which are transferred to the characters from the author herself. We are back, that is, to 'real life'. Exaggeration there is, but rarely disproportion. Charlotte Brontë gives us real life heightened. Sometimes the incident appears bizarre, but the essence is always true.

List of Charlotte Brontë's works

(Note: Charlotte Brontë used the name of 'Currer Bell' as a pseudonym.)

Poems by Currer, Ellis and Acton Bell, 1846.
Jane Eyre, An Autobiography, edited by Currer Bell, 3 vols., 1847.
Shirley, A Tale, by Currer Bell, 3 vols., 1849.
Villette, by Currer Bell, 3 vols., 1853.
The Professor, A Tale, by Currer Bell, 2 vols., 1857 (preface by A. B. Nicholls).
'*Emma*', *Cornhill Magazine*, April 1860 [A fragment].
The Novels and Poems of Charlotte, Emily and Anne Brontë, 7 vols., 1901–07 (World's Classics).
The Complete Poems of Charlotte Brontë, ed. C. K. Shorter & C. W. Hatfield, 1923.

These last two provide reliable modern editions of C.B.'s work. The three main novels are also published by Dent in the Everyman edition.

Letters

The Brontes: Their Lives, Friendships and Correspondence, ed. T. J. Wise and J. A. Symington, 8 vols., Oxford: Blackwell, Shakespeare Head Press, 1932–8.

Lesser Works

(Until the appearance of Shorter and Hatfield's edition of the poems noted above Shorter and, less often, T. J. Wise published Charlotte

Brontë's works in small privately printed editions. A few prose fragments were also published, but the main work on the Angrian writings, which deal with the fantasy world of the Brontë children's creating, is that by Ratchford and de Vere noted below. This did not appear until 1933. In the following entries *BST* indicates transactions of the Brontë Society.)

The Adventures of Ernest Alembert, A Fairy Tale, ed. T. J. Wise, 1896 (privately printed), (also in *Literary Anecdotes of the Nineteenth Century*, ed. Sir W. R. Nicoll and T. J. Wise, Vol. II, 1896).

The Moores [A fragment printed with *Jane Eyre*, ed. Sir W. R. Nicoll, 1902.]

Richard Coeur de Lion and Blondell, A Poem, ed. C. K. Shorter, 1912 (privately printed).

The Love Letters of Charlotte Brontë to Constantin Heger, ed. M. H. Spielmann, *Times*, 29 July 1913.

Saul and other Poems, 1913 (privately printed).

Lament befitting these 'Times of Night', ed. G. E. MacLean, *Cornhill Magazine*, August 1916.

Unpublished Essays in Novel Writing by Charlotte Brontë, ed. G. E. MacLean, 1916.

The Violet. A Poem written at the age of fourteen, ed. C. K. Shorter [1916] (privately printed).

The Red Cross Knight and other Poems, 1917 (privately printed).

The Swiss Emigrant's Return and other Poems, 1917 (privately printed).

The Four Wishes, A Fairy Tale, ed. C. K. Shorter, 1918 (privately printed).

Latest Gleanings: being a Series of Unpublished Poems from Early Manuscripts, ed. C. K. Shorter, 1918 (privately printed).

Napoleon and the Spectre, A Ghost Story, 1919 (privately printed). Extracted from 'The Green Dwarf'. See *Legends of Angria* below.

Darius Codomannus, A Poem, written at the age of eighteen years, 1920 (privately printed).

An Early Essay by Charlotte Brontë, ed. M. H. Spielmann, 1924.

Conversations (A Dialogue Playlet in Prose and Verse), ed. D. Cook, *Bookman*, December 1925.

The Twelve Adventures and other Stories, ed. C. K. Shorter, 1925.

Miniature Magazines of Charlotte Brontë, with Unpublished Poems, ed. D. Cook, *Bookman*, December 1926.

The Spell, an Extravaganza, ed. G. E. MacLean, 1931.

Legends of Angria, compiled from the Early Writings of Charlotte Brontë, ed. F. E. Ratchford and W. C. de Vere, New Haven: Yale University Press, 1933. Contains 'The Green Dwarf', 'Zamorna's Exile', 'Mina Laury', 'Caroline Vernon', 'Farewell to Angria'.

Unpublished Manuscripts, *BST*, VIII, 1933.

LIST OF CHARLOTTE BRONTË'S WORKS

Two Unpublished Poems by Charlotte Brontë, *BST*, VII, 1931.
Two Unpublished MSS. foreshadowing *Villette*, *BST*, VII, 1931.
Review at Gazemba: Lines, previously unpublished, by Charlotte Brontë, *BST*, VIII, 1934.
The Story of Willie Ellin: Fragments of an unfinished novel by Charlotte Brontë, *BST*, IX, 1936.
A Charlotte Brontë Manuscript [Second Series of *Youngman's Magazine*, No. 1, 1830], ed. C. M. Edgerley, *BST*, X, 1941.
A Frenchman's Journal: a Charlotte Brontë Manuscript, ed. C. M. Edgerley, *BST*, X, 1942.
Four Essays by Charlotte Brontë, *BST* XII, 1952.
Two Letters from Charlotte Brontë to Mrs. Gaskell, *BST*, XII, 1952.

Bibliography

A Bibliography of the Writings of the Brontës, by T. J. Wise. 1917 (privately printed); reprinted 1965.

Select bibliography

A Biography

GASKELL, MRS. E. C., *Life of Charlotte Brontë*, London: Smith Elder, 1857. One of the great Victorian biographies. A most sympathetic presentation, with extensive quotations from letters. Edited by May Sinclair (Everyman), 1908.

SHORTER, C. K., *The Brontës and Their Circle*, London: Hodder & Stoughton, 1896. *The Brontës: Life and Letters*, London: Hodder & Stoughton, 2 vols. 1908. The latter is an extension of the former and held the field in Brontë biographical scholarship until Wise and Symington's work appeared in 1932.

SINCLAIR, M., *The Three Brontës*, London: Hutchinson, 1912; revised 1914. A very readable account.

WISE, T. J. AND SYMINGTON, J. A., *The Brontës: Their Lives, Friendships and Correspondence*, Oxford: Blackwell, Shakespeare Head Press, 8 vols., 1932–8. Collects the Brontë correspondence and arranges it to form an extensive biographical survey.

HANSON, L. AND E. M., *The Four Brontës*, London: Oxford University Press, 1949.

LANE, MARGARET, *The Brontë Story*, London: Heinemann, 1953. A reconsideration of Mrs. Gaskell's *Life*.

GÉRIN, W., *Charlotte Brontë, the Evolution of Genius*, London: Oxford University Press, 1967. Carefully documented. Especially valuable for the Brussels period and Charlotte's relations with her publishers.

Recent studies of the other Brontës include:

GÉRIN, W., *Bramwell Brontë*, London: Nelson, 1961. *Anne Brontë*, London: Nelson, 1959.

SELECT BIBLIOGRAPHY

HOPKINS, A. B., *The Father of the Brontës*, London : Oxford University Press, and Baltimore : John Hopkins University Press, 1958.
LOCK, J. AND DIXON, W. T., *A Man of Sorrow*, London : Nelson, 1965
Both these on Patrick Brontë.

B Criticism

There have been few full-length studies, but mention may be made of the following :

RATCHFORD, F. E., *The Brontës' Web of Childhood*, London : Oxford University Press, and New York: Columbia University Press, 1941. On the childhood writings of the Brontës.

DRY, F. S., *The Sources of Jane Eyre*, Cambridge : Heffer, 1940.
MARTIN, R. B., *The Accents of Persuasion*, London : Faber, 1966. An extended and very competent examination of the novels.
EWBANK, I-S., *Their Proper Sphere*, London : Arnold, 1966. A study of all three Brontës as essentially Victorian female novelists.

C General Studies

SHEPHEARD, H., *A Vindication of the Clergy Daughters' School from the Remarks in the Life of Charlotte Brontë*, Kirkby Lonsdale : R. Morphet, and London : Seeley, Jackson and Halliday, 1857. A defence of Carus Wilson by his son-in-law against Mrs. Gaskell's criticisms.
Transactions and Publications of the Brontë Society, 1895 to date.
WOOD, T. B., (ed.), *Charlotte Brontë 1816–1916: A Centenary Memorial*, London : Unwin [1918]. Contains articles by Edmund Gosse, G. K. Chesterton, Halliwell Sutcliffe, Richard Garnett and others.
BENTLEY, P., *The Brontës*, London : Wingate, 1949. *The Brontë Sisters*, London : British Council, 1950. This latter appears in the British Council series 'Writers and Their Work' and contains a good bibliography.

Contemporary Reviews

[LEWES, G. H.] *Frazer's Magazine*, 36, 1847 [on *Jane Eyre*]. *Edinburgh Review*, 91, 1850. [on *Shirley*].
EASTLAKE, LADY, *Quarterly Review*, December 1848 [on *Jane Eyre* and *Vanity Fair*].

Comment in Books

STEPHEN, L., *Hours in a Library*, Vol. 3, London : Smith, Elder, 1879. Chapter on Charlotte Brontë.

BALD, M. A., *Women Writers of the Nineteenth Century*, London: Cambridge University Press, 1923. Somewhat pedestrian consideration.

WOOLF, VIRGINIA, *The Common Reader*, London: Hogarth Press, 1925. Remarks on *Jane Eyre* and *Wuthering Heights*.

CECIL, DAVID, *Early Victorian Novelists*, London: Constable, 1934; revised 1964. Perceptive chapter, but not always sympathetic.

TINKER, C. B., *Essays in Retrospect*, London: Oxford University Press, and New Haven: Yale University Press, 1948. Chapter on The Poetry of the Brontës.

O'CONNOR, W. VAN (ed.), *Forms of Modern Fiction*, London: Cambridge University Press, and Chicago: Chicago University Press, 1948. Essay by R. Chase on 'The Brontës, or Myths Domesticated'. Has been described as 'socio-psychological speculation'.

TILLOTSON, KATHLEEN, *Novels of the Eighteen-Forties*, Oxford: Clarendon Press, 1954. Chapter on *Jane Eyre* and wide-ranging introduction on the novel in these years.

RATHBONE, R. C. AND STEINMANN, M. (ed.), *From Jane Austen to Joseph Conrad*, London: Oxford University Press and Minneapolis: University of Minnesota Press, 1958. Contains R. B. Heilman's stimulating 'Charlotte Brontë's "New" Gothic'.

SHAPIRO, C. (ed.), *Twelve Original Essays on Great English Novels*, Detroit: Wayne State University Press, 1958. Includes '*Jane Eyre*: A Romantic Exemplum with a Difference' by J. Prescott.

Articles in Periodicals

RATCHFORD, F. E., 'Charlotte Brontë's Angrian Cycle of Stories', *PMLA*, XLIII, 1928. 'The Brontës' Web of Dreams', *Yale Review*, XXI, 1931.

WARD, B., 'Charlotte Brontë and the World of 1846', *BST* XI, 1946.

MASON, L., 'Charlotte Brontë and Charles Dickens', *Dickensian* XLIII, 1947.

SCARGILL, M. H., 'All Passion Spent: A Revaluation of *Jane Eyre*', *University of Toronto Quarterly*, XIX, 1950.

MARTIN, R. B., 'Charlotte Brontë and Harriet Martineau', *Nineteenth Century Fiction*, VII, 1952.

SHANNON, JNR., E. F., 'The Present Tense in *Jane Eyre*', *Nineteenth Century Fiction*, X, 1955.

KORG, J., 'The Problem of Unity in *Shirley*', *Nineteenth Century Fiction*, XII, 1957.

BRIGGS, A., 'Private and Social Themes in *Shirley*', *BST*, XIII, 1958.

HEILMAN, R. B., 'Charlotte Brontë, Reason and the Moon', *Nineteenth Century Fiction*, XIV, 1960.

COLBY, R. A., '*Villette* and the Life of the Mind', *PMLA*, LXXV, 1960.

SELECT BIBLIOGRAPHY

BURKHART, C., 'Another Key Word for *Jane Eyre*', *Nineteenth Century Fiction*, XVI, 1961.

MARSHALL, W. H., 'The Self, the World and the Structure of *Jane Eyre*', *Revue des langues vivantes*, V, 1961.

HUGHES, F. E., 'Jane Eyre, the unbaptised Dionysus', *Nineteenth Century Fiction*, XVIII, 1964.

Manuscripts

The MS. of *The Professor* is in the Pierpont Morgan Library, New York, and the holographs of the other three novels are in the British Museum.